My Father
Who Is on Earth

by

John Lloyd Wright

A New Edition

INCLUDING COMMENTS, RESPONSES, AND DOCUMENTS

BY

Frank Lloyd Wright

AND

John Lloyd Wright

Edited with an Introduction by
Narciso G. Menocal

Postscript by
Elizabeth Wright Ingraham

Southern Illinois University Press
Carbondale and Edwardsville

Notes and comments of Frank Lloyd Wright and John Lloyd Wright are
reprinted by permission of Avery Architectural and Fine Arts Library,
Columbia University in the City of New York and copyrighted by
The Frank Lloyd Wright Foundation

Printed in the United States of America

Edited by Robyn Laur Clark

Designed by Bob Nance

Production supervised by Natalia Nadraga

97 96 95 94   4 3 2 1

Library of Congress Cataloging-in-Publication Data

Wright, John Lloyd.
    My father who is on earth / John Lloyd Wright. — New ed. / including
comments, responses, and documents by Frank Lloyd Wright and John
Lloyd Wright; edited and with an introduction by Narciso G. Menocal;
postscript by Elizabeth Wright Ingraham.
        p.   cm.
    1. Wright, Frank Lloyd, 1867–1959. 2. Architects — United
States — Biography.   I. Wright, Frank Lloyd, 1867–1959.   II. Menocal,
Narciso G.   III. Ingraham, Elizabeth Wright.   IV. Title.
    NA737.W7W7   1994
    720′.92 — dc20
    [B]   92-1316
    ISBN 0-8093-1749-4   CIP

Frontispiece: Frank Lloyd Wright and John Lloyd Wright.
Courtesy of Avery Library Architectural and Fine Arts Library,
Columbia University in the City of New York.

The paper used in this publication meets the minimum requirements
of American National Standard for Information Sciences — Permanence
of Paper for Printed Library Materials, ANSI Z39.48-1984. ♾

Contents

Foreword

SOMETIME DURING THE 1960s John Lloyd Wright approached Avery Library with a list of books and documents in his possession that he was offering for possible sale. Among these only one of the three copies of *My Father Who Is on Earth* that are here published was listed. This was the one returned by "Dad" on 2 April 1946 with marginal comments in his own hand. Adolf K. Placzek, then Avery Librarian, visited John and his wife Frances in their splendid home in Del Mar, California, and they took an instant liking to each other. The correspondence files in Avery attest to a lasting and warm friendship. There are letters about visits and about various purchases of those things Avery needed and could afford to buy, interspersed with records of generous donations of other items John Lloyd Wright decided to part with.

During 1971 they discussed the possibility of having Columbia University Press publish a facsimile of the annotated copy of *My Father Who Is on Earth*, but nothing seems to have come of it. Upon John's death in 1972, after a heartfelt letter of condolence, Placzek suggested to Wright's widow, Frances, that it might be appropriate for her to donate the document to Avery, but apparently she too was reluctant. It is in a letter she wrote to Dolf Placzek, dated 27 December 1973, that she first mentions the existence of another copy, in which, she says "John replied in each page to everything Father Wright wrote in his copy."

But no mention is made of a third copy, containing notes and additions in preparation for a new edition that was to have its title altered, significantly, to *Frank Lloyd Wright: As I Knew Him*, until Judge Louis M. Welsh sent me a list of the materials in his possession with a letter dated 25 April 1983, addressed to the Avery Librarian. In it he briefly tells about the fondness his late mother and stepfather had for Avery and Adolf K. Placzek and of his own intention to donate the annotated copy of *My Father Who Is on Earth*. One of Placzek's last letters before his retirement in 1980 had been to Judge Welsh making inquiries about the book.

It has been my good fortune to have inherited not only the extraordinary collections of Avery Library but the good will engendered by my predecessor wherever he went. A previously scheduled visit to California afforded me the opportunity to pay Judge Welsh a visit. I was warmly received by Louis and his wife Pat in the same splended house in Del Mar where Placzek had met its talented architect, John Lloyd Wright. I well remember the warmth of that fall afternoon and the terrace enhanced by a spectacular array of cineraria plants grown by the deft hands of Pat Welsh. I left in awe, with my heart full of joy and my arms full of treasures entrusted to me for eventual addition to Avery Library, the most precious being the three copies of *My Father Who Is on Earth*.

Judge Welsh's list was impressive. It included some items from the original list of John Lloyd Wright, filling the gaps. But it also included some new things, among them a delicate envelope hand printed by Frank Lloyd Wright with a title that read "Hill Side Home School: Collection of

Views," possibly designed as a scrapbook enclosure for collecting material about the school run by two of Frank Lloyd Wright's aunts, and an annual report of the same school in which the photo of John (called then John Kenneth Wright) appears along with that of his brother Frank Lloyd Wright, Jr. (later in life known as Lloyd). There was also a manuscript entitled "Special Problems That Befall a Son of a Great Man."

Louis and Pat Welsh visited Avery in April 1984 and during a luncheon with Dolf and Beverly Placzek, the Judge announced his intention to donate all the materials he had sent to Avery in honor of Adolf K. Placzek, for which we all duly celebrated.

One of the rare pleasures of librarianship is to bring books and people together. The book now being published began by recounting a story of separation between father and son. It gives me great pleasure to see them brought together in these pages, with the added perspective of a third generation of this most extraordinary American architectural dynasty, and I am grateful to Narciso G. Menocal and Southern Illinois University Press for making it possible.

—ANGELA GIRAL *Avery Librarian*

Introduction

THE STORY OF THE PRESENT EDITION OF *My Father Who Is on Earth* began a few years ago when Angela Giral, having just become director of the Avery Library of Columbia University and knowing my interest in Frank Lloyd Wright, informed me that Judge Louis M. Welsh, John Lloyd Wright's stepson, had given the library a collection of his stepfather's papers. Among them were the copies of *My Father Who Is on Earth* from which the present edition developed.

The story is a complicated one. On 29 March 1946, the day of publication, John sent his father a copy of the book. Upon receiving it, Frank Lloyd Wright penciled his comments on the margins of most pages and returned the book to John. On 14 April John sent his father a second copy with his father's comments transcribed in black pencil and his answers to them written in red pencil. Along with the book, he sent the following note:

> You asked for another book, Dad—so I send it. In it the real John speaks his real reason for writing the book—in the silence of the penciled lines—marked on the opus—itself.
>
> When you read the book again, I am sure you will like it,—even more?
>
> Affectionately,
John 4.14.46

Publication date March 29th, 1946

Before sending his father the second copy of the book (and to complete his records), John transcribed all comments to a third copy, differentiating his from his father's once more with red and black pencils. That third copy is the basis of the present publication.

Frank Lloyd Wright had been waiting for this book with some trepidation. A year earlier, on 6 March 1945, he had written his son: "Dear John: What is this talk of a book? Of all that I don't need and dread is more exploitation. Can't you drop it?" and signed, "FLLW ergo your Dad."

On the twelfth, John responded:

The book, "My Father Who Is On Earth" by John Lloyd Wright will put a stop to exploitation. Need I recall that your Oak Park batch of children have never exploited you, rather, perhaps, they have been exploited[?]

You will like the book, and as I told you twenty months ago, it will be good for you. [Therefore, July 1943, perhaps the time for the first idea for the book.] Just think, for three dollars and fifty cents you can come upon the "things I really grew up with." Now come on with the photograph of the man with the magnificent ego and sweet sentimentality. I'll tell you again, I'm proud of my Papa. [And signed the letter,] John, the Lloyd Wright, ergo your son.

In late July 1985 I made a special trip to New York to transcribe onto an enlarged photocopy of *My Father* the glosses in black and red pencil. At that time I also saw in

Avery another copy of *My Father* with John's emendations for a never-published edition that was to bear the title of *Frank Lloyd Wright: As I Knew Him*. This work was done after Frank Lloyd Wright's death. On page 4, on the copyright line, John inserted the year 1962 after 1946 and referred to his father's death in the typescript of an addendum. In addition to the addendum, there was also a foreword and three textual insertions, published herein. Only minor corrections have been made in order not to disturb the sense of the original.

The file on *My Father* remained in my study more as a curiosity than anything else until one day I mentioned it to Kenney Withers, former director of Southern Illinois University Press, during the course of a casual conversation at a Frank Lloyd Wright symposium at the University of Michigan. He became enthusiastic about publishing a new edition of *My Father* with the comments. Elizabeth Wright Ingraham, John's daughter, supported the project and very graciously offered her own comments, which we have great pleasure in publishing. To round out the story, we are also publishing a paper by John Lloyd Wright entitled "Problems That Befall a Son of a Great Man." It is dated 5 July 1957, and it is an early version of "In My Father's Shadow," an article published in *Esquire* 49 (February 1958), 55–57.

We are most grateful to Ms. Ingraham for her cooperation, to the Taliesin Fellowship for allowing us to publish the texts written by Frank Lloyd Wright and for supplying replacement photos for some of the illustrations, to the Graduate School of the University of Wisconsin-Madison for supporting the project with a grant, to the Avery Library, Columbia

INTRODUCTION

University, and most especially to its director, Angela Giral, for splendid support of this project.

Frank Lloyd Wright's name would appear even on the shortest list of major twentieth-century architects. His son's, John Lloyd Wright, also an architect (born 12 December 1892, died 20 December 1972), appears only in specialized monographs, and then, directly or indirectly, implied or explicitly, as "the son of."[1] That difference between father and son cursed John's life, especially since his father fostered it. In the *Esquire* magazine article John said of his father: "I once heard him say to one of *my* clients, 'Why fool around with the coupon when you can have the genuine bond?' " And yet, John loved his father intensely, so much so that twelve years earlier he wrote *My Father Who Is on Earth*.

The book, then, is about an unresolved conflict, about the anger of a son toward a father who imposed his own idea of perfection upon his children, as an extension of his ego. There is also a son's natural tenderness for his father, as well as his admiration for his father's intellectual and artistic ability. The book was John's catharsis. The main character may have been godlike, "like the vulnerable actor, who, whenever he hears a clap of thunder, strides majestically to the window and proceeds to take a bow," John noted in the *Esquire* piece. But concurrently, that character was very

1. The best assessment of John Lloyd Wright's life and work is Ann Van Zanten, "John Lloyd Wright: Architecture and Design," in Sally Kitt Chappell and Ann Van Zanten, *Barry Byrne, John Lloyd Wright: Architecture and Design* (Chicago: Chicago Historical Society, 1982), 41–71.

much on earth, with all the failings that such a condition entails. In the end, John, the son of the famous man, resolved the conflict by forgiving his father for not having been a genius in all human categories instead of just one.

Born John Kenneth Wright on 12 December 1892 in his father's Oak Park house, John changed his middle name to Lloyd when he began to work as an architect, thus, paradoxically—as well as revealingly—identifying himself with the father from whom he wished to be differentiated. To the end, John concealed the fact that he had changed his name. He ended his *Esquire* article by saying: "But until such time as society shall come to have faith in *both the father and the son*, I am fated to be known by the general public not as John Lloyd Wright, my christened name, but as Frank Lloyd Wright's son, my given name. It is a birthmark which I have learned to bear proudly, letting the quips fall where they may."

But "the quips" came only with adulthood. The trite adjective "golden" characterizes John's childhood and early youth. In *My Father* he tells us of the revelry of a child who would stand on the balcony above the heads of his father's draftsmen and throw things at them only to have his father come and with great laughter chase him, catch him, perch him on his shoulders, and ride him back to Mother. There was a ten-year-old child's innocently wicked fun in watching "the naked woman" his father kept on the drawing room balcony (the model Richard Bock used for the statue of *Flower in the Crannied Wall*). There were also dozens of colored balloons his father would release at a time in the magically beautiful playroom of the house, which he—the father—would rearrange and play with by the hour. There was a horse for each of the children, and also, at one time, a burglar for whom "Papa turned on the lights so that he [the burglar] could see better." Above all, there was the father's unending, contagious laughter, a laughter that one night, at a theater, prompted a comedian to bow in tribute to the elder Wright. There was also a seemingly endless stream of parties, "clambakes . . . in his studio, cotillions in the larger drafting room; gay affairs about the blazing logs that snapped and crackled in the big fireplace. From week to week, month to month, our home was a round of parties. There were parties somewhere all of the time and everywhere some of the time." And then, there was the architecture. John tells us of his aesthetic experience the first time that he entered the Piazza San Marco in Venice. He went in through a narrow entrance and the square opened on to him like a blossom. It was the same feeling he sensed the first day he came into the kindergarten room in his Oak Park house. The aesthetic experience extended into his aunts' Hillside Home School as well, which he attended. But when John was but sixteen came the debacle: Wright left for good with Mrs. Cheney. "I let it go as something I could not understand," John wrote. "I knew I would have to adjust my own life, and I've been doing so ever since." The golden age was over.

In 1911, after a short stint at the University of Wisconsin — which his father and brother also had attended — John moved to San Diego; University authorities had suggested that he might wish to forego his studies in view of his poor academic performance. After a number of odd jobs — including pressing pants in a laundry (at which he failed) — John went into architecture, signing first as draftsman with a residential contractor, and subsequently, in 1912, with the firm of Harrison Albright, where he built his first commission, the Wood house in Escondido, an elaboration of his father's 1906 design for the Grace Fuller house, Glencoe, Illinois. John became so irrevocably his father's son that a year later he was the head of Wright's architecture office at Orchestra Hall, Chicago, during the commission of Midway Gardens. At this point one gets an important insight into his father's conception of an architectural education. He presented John with a copy of Viollet-le-Duc's *Discourses on Architecture* (where "you will find all the architecture schooling you will ever need") and with the by now famous dictum "five lines where three are enough is stupidity. Nine pounds where three are sufficient is obesity. To know what to leave out and what to put in, just where and just how . . . is to have been educated in knowledge of simplicity." While the chapter on Midway Gardens does not give us any clue concerning the organization of and everyday practice in Frank Lloyd Wright's office during the crucial years when he was commuting between Chicago and Taliesin (where he lived with Mamah Borthwick Cheney), John does give us important information on two accounts. He describes how his father designed Midway Gardens in one Zen-like burst of creativity, transferring the complete design, including dimensions, from the mind's eye to the paper at one sitting (very much like Edgar Tafel later described the design of Fallingwater). The second important account is that of the Taliesin murders in August 1914, especially since John accompanied his father all of the time during those troubled days.

After a two-page chapter on his mother, where in one sentence John perhaps explains the main, deeper reason for the rift between the Wrights and Frank's turning to Mamah Borthwick ("had Mother been able to direct the lives of others at all times—I don't doubt that everything would have been forever beautiful"), he proceeds on to a chapter on the Imperial Hotel in Tokyo, where, regretfully, he is more autobiographical than biographical. He tells us next to nothing about the process of design and construction of the commission. Instead, he goes into a narrative of his father's parsimony concerning payments and how he had to collect his salary from a payment Viscount Inouye had made for designs for a house Wright designed and John drafted. The subtraction of his salary from the commission was, allegedly, the cause for being fired by his father. Or so John wrote. The truth was different, and we are grateful to Ms. Ingraham for setting the record straight in this volume's Postscript.

Back in Chicago in 1918, John sought work from Louis Sullivan, but realizing that Sullivan had no work, he traded him one of his jigsawed storks for a design for an ashtray that was never manufactured. Unfortunately, Sullivan's drawing was lost later in a fire. This was at the time when John patented his famous Lincoln Logs, which he had invented in Japan in 1917 and then sold through Marshall Field's.

And so ends what one may call the first half of *My Father Who Is on Earth*, covering the period in which John depended on his father either as parent or employer, and one is not sure of much of a distinction between the two conditions. Curiously—or just perhaps because this book is not about Frank Lloyd Wright, but about John's father—the author does not go into his father's post-Imperial hotel work, but then, in 1945, when he wrote this book, he might have thought that Hitchcock's *In the Nature of Materials* (1942) had covered the ground.

In the rest of the book—chapters 14–21—John tells us what he thought was extraordinary about his father. But perhaps that assessment is not quite right. It might be best to say that the rest of the book is about what John saw as his father's contribution to his son's character. While *My Father Who Is on Earth* is about the private persona of Frank Lloyd Wright, that persona turns out to be the writer's own existential image, a trope standing for a personal ideal. All the values that John accepted from his father are there; all the flaws that John rejected from his father are also there; and the difference between value and flaw is entirely subjective.

The most useful section in this part of the book is perhaps when John tells us about his father's method of design. "Where creative effort is involved," Wright liked to say, "there are no trivial circumstances." This statement was to John at the core of his father's "heroic quest" of organic architecture, and he tells us how his father took into consideration the secondary as much as the important, bringing every scintilla to contribute to the building, always bearing in mind the joy of the client in making use of a thing of beauty. Yet, paradoxically, this was done mostly in Wright's terms, seldom the client's.

Through somewhat lengthy quotations, John attempted to show how organic architecture originated with Viollet-le-Duc, in his and his father's opinion. John sums up the argument (and the "genealogy") by saying: "We can look to the great teacher, Viollet-le-Duc; to the great master Louis H. Sullivan; to the great designer, Frank Lloyd Wright, who embraced the ideals of the teacher and . . . the inspiration of the master." Later John changed the sentence around in a manner that is quite revealing of his feelings to his father. "We can look to the master architect Frank Lloyd Wright, who embraced the ideals of the greater teacher E. Viollet-le-Duc, and with the inspiration of his master Louis Sullivan." As an assertion of his father's ideas on organic architecture, John inserted the text of *The House Beautiful*, William C. Gannett's Unitarian sermon on the aestheticization of life, which Wright and William Winslow printed as a book in 1896 and which served by much as the source of many of Wright's ideas on the relationship of family behavior and the home, a relationship that was very much at the core of his concept of residential architecture.

Finally, in the last two chapters, John rebuked his father. He based his text on the fortieth chapter of the Book of Isaiah, a favorite text among the Lloyd Jones, but which his father disliked since he considered Isaiah as a monster who made God different from earthly beauty. (The eighth verse was the most offending: "The grass withereth, the flower fadeth: but the word of our God shall stand for ever.")

John insisted that "Isaiah's O.K., Dad" (the title of his chapter 19) and said so on the strength of his father being a kind of Isaiah incarnate, deprecating, and even riving when he could, everything and everyone standing in the path of his beliefs, especially those pertaining to architecture. In John's opinion, his father simply misunderstood Isaiah. In the last chapter John placed his father in a dream in which the elder Wright arrived in heaven to be told that, in fact, in an earlier life he had been Isaiah—as well as Voltaire (whom John placed as contemporaneous with Louis XIV) and Rousseau. St. Peter then tells Wright that he will not be allowed to redesign Heaven, a point in the narrative that John used to criticize his father's inability to accept other people's views, not allowing even his disciples to bloom into their own. Yet, John's love for his father is ever-present in the book. At the end, when Wright wakes up, John is there, and both go forth to build Broadacre City, the model of Wright's utopian world.

The book, therefore, ends with the same unresolved conflict of emotions with which it began. That conflict was never solved, as attested by the 1958 *Esquire* article and by the two documents that John later added to the text. To the end—and even perhaps in his own existential knowledge of himself—John was plagued with his position as "the son of."

—NARCISO G. MENOCAL

Textual Note

The main text of this volume is a reprint of the 1946 edition of *My Father Who Is on Earth*, with notes, comments, and corrections made by John Lloyd Wright and Frank Lloyd Wright. All glosses have been placed in the margins as close as possible to the passages to which they refer. Each is marked [JLLW] for John Lloyd Wright or [FLLW] for Frank Lloyd Wright. Occasional editorial explications are marked [Editor]. Minor typographical errors have been silently corrected.

That text is followed by John Lloyd Wright's 1962 additions for a new, albeit unpublished edition of *My Father*. This new material consists of a foreword, three textual insertions, and an addendum.

"Special Problems That Befall a Son of a Great Man," dated 5 July 1957, by John Lloyd Wright, comes next. This is an earlier, fuller version of "In My Father's Shadow," an article that appeared in *Esquire* 49 (February 1958), 55–57.

Originals of all these writings are deposited in Avery Library, Columbia University.

MY FATHER WHO IS ON EARTH

[JLLW] Dad wrote:

"Dear John: Herewith ungracious comments marked on the opus-itself—as I read.

Kindly send me another one—will you? Hope you and Frances are happy and get some money as well as fun out of it all—

Love—

Dad

Frank Lloyd Wright

April 2nd, 1946
Scotsdale (sic)
Arizona

MY FATHER WHO IS ON EARTH

JOHN LLOYD WRIGHT

If the characters in this book resemble in any way, anyone living or dead—it is meant that they should do so. *

*[FLLW] And John—they do, in a way quite your own—Yes, I appreciate the affection you express for your next-to-the-principal character—(for I share it for you) but—of all your "characters" I think you have done the principal one—(yourself)—best—And this is *as autobiography ought to be*—else why the thing at all—? Unless for money—? There is some truth in it, tho—And "Dad" hopes you will get some money out of this—(On the whole) a well-written washing of family linen—soiled—but not so dirty as one might think?—I think your book will sell . . . Whistler once called attention to the fact that he could take care of his enemies but prayed the Lord to deliver him from his friends—and this being nearer than "friends" is that much worse—for me? Yes? As the plot thickens, life grows more interesting—however. Yes?

Dad.

my wife, Frances, "the Priestess" so named by Dad; a beautifully proportioned soul, without whom this book would not have been written.

Dear Dad,

Maybe you did not ask to read the manuscript for this book because you felt, as I did, that this would not have been in harmony with the independence which has been our practice.

After I got off my mind everything—or almost everything I wanted to say, I suddenly felt alone and on my own—for I thought of your recent note in which you wrote, "I'm a little gun shy on this publicity business but the affectionate father of son John just the same—" I rushed to the Duneland retreat of your good friend Ferdinand Schevill, knowing him to be a gentle soul of great compassion, and asked him to read the manuscript.

"Come on with it," said Dr. Schevill, "your father may not like everything in it, but why should he?"

Well—anyway, anyhow—here it is.

Fifty years from the time I first became conscious of you, I give you you in one book that you have not read before.

Let it be, affectionately, from Frances and me. And Dad— if you read it and come upon shadows, remember—sunshine made them.

Your son John.

FOREPART

TO WRITE truthfully about any man and his accomplishments, it is necessary to know that the source of his inspiration comes from the One Source which is available to all. In delving into the life of my father, as well as into the lives of those masters from whom he derived inspiration, this truth becomes clear. I now see the Architect and the Father, two men in one body. Through the years an inherent lack of interdependence between us has allowed such a perspective. I can see him through the eyes of a contemporary architect as well as through the eyes of a son.

On occasions in the last several years, I have sent Dad a book that I enjoyed, thinking he too would find some pleasure in reading. His invariable reply is something like this: ". . . I wonder why you come so late in life upon things you really grew up with. . . ." Just an appreciative soul writing a thank-you note.*

Since he wrote in his Autobiography that the real book is between the lines, I wrote him a note: ". . . I am writing a book between the lines. I will probably call it A *Son's Eye View of His Dad*, or *My Father on Earth in Heaven and in Hell*. Please send me a list of your honors and an up-to-date photograph of your royal likeness. . . ." To this he replied: ". . . I hope you are not writing a book wherein I cut

*[FLLW] "?" [Editor] FLLW added a question mark to the sentence "Just an appreciative soul writing a thank-you note."

9

much of a figure. . . ." To that I replied: ". . . I feel for your hope. The book will be good for you, serve you right and you'll like it. It will reap up the past, lay hold of the present, grab on to the future. In it I will forgive you for everything I've done. At least it will be one book I can give you that you have not read before. But cheer up! 'The Priestess' with her delicate but strong hand will hold mine while I write. I am sure that will save both of us and the book." In due time, a heavy manuscript, in which his honors were listed, and an up-to-date photograph arrived.

In our early family years the name Papa was a traditional form which we later outgrew. Dad says the word Papa was offensive to him, accent long on the first "a" making a more offensive word. The stuffy domesticity of the word applied to the male made it intolerable to him. I think it was only after he left home that the name Papa became intolerable. He seemed to like it in the days we used it, or else he suffered in silence. Therefore—Papa is used now only where it was a part of him then.

I need not introduce you to the Architect. He has made a good job of that himself. But since the Architect in the Father cannot be entirely detached, I bring in the Architect. Yet, it is more particularly the Father in the Architect—the villain who is the hero of this tale—of whom I write. So, between the lines with me, meet Papa, Dad, in *My Father Who Is on Earth*.

John Lloyd Wright

At Long Beach, Indiana

PARTS

MY FATHER WHO IS ON EARTH

1. IN THE BEGINNING

"AINT'S REST" they called it—better known as Oak Park, Illinois. Amid patriarch trees on the low-rolling land, his nearest neighbor a church a mile away, Frank Lloyd Wright conceived something new in the building of his time. And he started with the building of his own house—a continuously mortgaged and periodically remodeled experimental laboratory of design and finance!

Horizontal lines; double-leveled rooms of one and two stories; scattered vases filled with leaves and wild flowers, massive fireplaces seemed to be everywhere. Here and there a Yourdes of rare beauty covered a floor. A Persian lantern, samovars, windows which met and turned the corners, lights filtering through fret-sawed ceiling grilles, sunshine and shadows . . . these made the house that was our home.

A woven fabric of brown creosoted cedar shingles was studded with diamond-leaded glass. Massive common brick walls were enriched by stone urns and Boston ivy. Covered screened porches overlooked terraced gardens, a pool and fountain in a garden court. All this grew naturally out of the luxuriant landscape.

The window and doorheads at the same level were connected by a continuous band. I remember a piano, a life-sized bronze bust of Beethoven, an old carved Chinese chair; "The Shere Mill Pond," a landscape by Turner, one by Wendt, statuettes of Indians by McNeil and some rare Kakemonos.

A gigantic willow tree grew right up through the roof of a corridor that connected the house with the large, two-story drafting room. Statuettes, wild flowers and leaves scattered the room in Dad's characteristic order. Here was inspiration, his inspiration, the kind which recognizes the beauty of the works of the past, yet lives in the world of today and cares for its simplest flowers.

The library was *books!* Long, thick, big, little books. Covers without books, books without covers; colored, patterned, and textured papers in large folios, all piled up and pushed on wide ledges on either side of a long window.

My first impression upon coming into the playroom from the narrow, long, low-arched, dimly lighted passageway that led to it was its great height and brilliant light. The ceiling twenty feet high formed a perfect arch springing from the heads of group windows which were recessed in Roman brick walls. The oak floor marked off with kindergarten arrangement of circles and squares was always strewn with queer dolls, building blocks, funny mechanical toys, animals that moved about and wagged their strange heads.

The semicircle plaster panel above the fireplace was covered by a mural of the allegorical "Fisherman and the Genie" designed by Dad and painted by Giannini. At night the flames from six-foot logs lit up strangely the serene face of the Genie and, at the opposite end, the Winged Victory over the door, making it stand out white and strong against the shadowy galleries beyond.

It was late one night, years later, when for the first time I came unexpectedly upon the Square of Saint Mark in Venice. After approaching through a narrow, low-arched passageway I found myself abruptly in the brightly lighted Square where a band concert had just been concluded. Walls of brick, sculptured balconies and niches, brilliant murals surrounded a multitude of brightly costumed people in picturesque confusion. Scores of white doves fluttered about. The sky formed an arched ceiling overhead. Only upon this one occasion did I ever have a similar impression to the one our playroom left with me. In this room were the milestones to maturity; treasures, friends, comrades, ambitions; and through the years I have dreamed through the inspiration of this playroom.

It was Dad's desire that his children should grow up with a recognition of what is good in the art of the house. He believed that an instinct for the beautiful would be firmly established by a room whose simple beauty and strength are daily factors. And Dad was right.

When I first became conscious of my father, he looked like this:

A self-photograph. No "picture-taker" could satisfy him. So he rigged up his camera with a long rubber tube, and at the right moment, squeezed the bulb! It was in the year 1895.

I looked like this:

He twenty-six, I three, this is evidence of what he did to me.
He wanted a girl, thus the dress and the curl! The tie is his.

His first design* looked like this:

*[Editor] This is neither Frank Lloyd Wright's first design nor is the date 1888. This is the Abraham Lincoln Center, Chicago, 1898. Dwight Heald Perkins (1867–1941) was Wright's associate architect.

Original design for Abraham Lincoln Center, Oakwood Boulevard in Chicago, made outside office hours in 1888, during the time he was chief draftsman for Adler and Sullivan.

Is it the Gay Nineties or 1946? Anachronism is the first thought that comes to mind when looking at this modern building in the midst of antiquated apparel and mode of travel. Yet it is not an anachronism. It simply conveys at a glance how far ahead of his time was the nineteen-year-old boy, Frank Lloyd Wright.*

The ideal of Jenkin Lloyd Jones, "Uncle Jenk" to us, was unity. His dream was to erect a building to house a social and civic center, and his nonsectarian church. He was the founder of All Souls Church in Chicago. His weekly publication was called *Unity*.

Here was an opportunity for one member of the family to allow expression for the rising genius of another member. So, Uncle Jenk commissioned "the boy" nephew to design the building.

Uncle Jenk and the trustees liked the design just as "the boy" made it, but Jenk was not so sure "the boy" was capable of carrying out so large a project. Then, too, Uncle Jenk knew that "the boy" had a mind of his own, equal to his in strength of will and determination. In keeping with the precedent of unity in family, everyone for himself, Uncle Jenk called in another architect whom he could direct, to collaborate with him and "the boy" in the building of "the boy's" design. Grossly offended, "the boy" would have nothing further to do with the project. Evidently this suited Uncle Jenk. He and his collaborator proceeded unhampered to carry out "the boy's" plan to suit themselves. The building emerged, a clumsily revised version of the original. The tradesmen called it "All Souls Cold Storage and Warehouse."

*[Editor] FLLW was born in 1867; the Abraham Lincoln Center was designed in 1898; therefore, he was 31, not 19.

*[JLLW] 1898

In 1893* he announced his practice like this:

A reproduction of the upper left-hand corner of the cover of a gray-paper, four-page brochure. The dark printing was Chinese red, the lighter black. His red-square mark shown above was later revised to a solid red square with single-line frame—then to a solid red square, unadorned. This is a characteristic note in his development toward simplicity.

A reproduction of the second page.

THE PRACTICE OF ARCHITECTURE as a profession has fine art as well as commercial elements.

These should be combined to their mutual benefit, not mixed to their detriment.

To develop in a better sense, this fine art side in combination with its commercial condition, the architect should place himself in an environment that conspires to develop the best there is in him. The first requisite is a place fitted and adapted to the work to be performed and set outside distractions of the busy city. The worker is enabled on this basis to secure the quiet concentration of effort essential to the full success of a building project,—the intrinsic value of which is measured by the quality of that effort.

To practice the profession of architecture along these lines, in the hope of reaching these better results, a complete architectural workshop has been constructed at Oak Park, and for purely business purposes, consultation and matters in connection with superintendence, an office has been located in "The Rookery," Chicago.

OFFICE HOURS: At 1119 Rookery from twelve to two, P. M. Telephone Main 2668. A record of work, together with plans and details in duplicate will be kept on file at this office and accessible to clients and contractors at this time.

At corner of Forest and Chicago Avenues, Oak Park: Eight to eleven, A. M. Seven to nine, P. M. Telephone Oak Park. Clients and those with a kindred interest in architecture will also be welcomed to the suburban studio during business hours, where provision has been made for their reception and entertainment.

The third page was a halftone paster of the plan and elevation of his studio. On the fourth page was printed:

"Oak Park may be reached by Lake Street elevated trains connecting at 48th Street with the Chicago Avenue surface electric road which passes the Studio, or by the Chicago and North-Western Ry."

He announced his first exhibition* like this:

*[JLLW] 1900 [Editor] subsequently JLLW wrote "1902?" and then marked it for deletion. The illustration is the cover of the 1902 Chicago Architectural Club exhibition catalogue.

The left-hand panel shows the sculptured capital with solemn secretary birds and open book beneath the fruitful tree.

The plan of his private study is etched on the pendant scroll. This enriched the square columns at the entrance to his studio. The chair on which stands the statuette goldenrod-holder of his red-haired boy John was the first piece of modern furniture made in this country.

Not satisfied with the bric-a-brac of the day, Father designed his own. The copper weed-holders pictured to the right and left of the chair are his early creations. Father liked weeds!

In those days furniture manufacturers would have nothing to do with furniture not of period design. Father didn't like periods! He designed most of our furniture and had it made in the mill where the doors and trim for his buildings were made. The pieces that were not built in, built out or nailed down, he rearranged with a regularity most disconcerting to Mother.

2. DAD THE PAPA

BROWN EYES full of love and mischief, a thick pompadour of dark wavy hair—that is my father when I think of him as he was when I was very young. His smile enlivened everything about him—his laugh defied grief and failure.

The unrestrained character of this man of Welsh and English ancestry, and his peculiarities of genius, caused him to have little in common with his neighbors. They thought him an eccentric visionary because his ideals and even the house that was our home were different from theirs. His clients were subjected to ridicule—a "crazy architect" built "freak houses" for them. He didn't think, act or dress like the fathers of the day, but was married like them and this, only, gave him a right to be at liberty.

His rebellion against existing conventional tyranny, his ardent temperament and headlong pursuit of whatever he most wanted not infrequently involved him in serious troubles from which, thanks to his own ingenuity and "good fairy," he emerged, scathed or unscathed—but he emerged!

As a young man he had the indispensable quality of confidence in himself. He was ambitious, but his idea of the way to rise was to improve himself, never suspecting that anyone wished to hinder him. And as for the ungenerous attempt to keep a young man down, he fought valiantly always, but never allowed his mind to be diverted from its true channel to brood over real or imaginary injuries.

He made sport of the inertia that blocks progress, and astonished everyone by his audacity. His outspokenness incurred both political and personal enmity. Yet his brilliant and attractive personality exercised a curious charm on those who knew him.

He bought my clothes, my shoes, my toys. He performed all the functions of fatherhood, only he performed them differently. He took no personal interest in my religious or academic training. But when it came to luxuries and play, he tenderly took my hand and led the way.

He performed all the functions of an architect, only he performed them differently.

He designed round drawers for square stationery!

He performed all the functions of an author, only he performed them differently.

He permitted no index in his books!

Not innocent of rudeness he boldly and knowingly broke the fetters of form. His devotion to his ideals caused his stubborn cry: "No Compromise"—his courage and love for his work, later, inspired in me the love for architecture.

He was the man whom I called Papa.

Papa went to bed late at night—pulled me under a cold shower with him in the morning—rubbed me with a coarse towel till my skin burned and glowed. He tickled my toes, tossed me into the air again and again to the accompaniment of my shrieks of delight and Mother's "Stop, Frank! Stop!"

I watched curiously as he laid off his dressing gown, put on his coat, arranged his flowing tie before the mirror—took a full breath of fresh air and led me down to Mother and to breakfast. Then he would disappear! That was the first great mystery of my life. Where did this man go, the man whom I called Papa?

I didn't see much of him except at mealtime until I was able to discover and find my way to the drafting room adjoining the house. Then the mystery was solved. I could get to the balcony from a hidden stairway. From here I would quietly throw things over the railing on the tops of the drafting tables and the heads of the drafting men. I saw more of him from then on. He would chase me, gather me up, perch me on his shoulder and ride me back to Mother. It wasn't long before he couldn't even catch me. He never punished me.

His favorite frolic was to torment me at mealtime. He would swing his arm over my head. I'd duck only to find he was scratching the back of his neck.

Now and then I wouldn't duck.

Now and then he'd pop me!

He bought colored gas balloons by the dozen—released them in the playroom—arranged and played with them by the hour.

Papa kept a naked woman on his drafting-room balcony. I saw her through the high windows opening over the flat gravel roof. She was pretty and had freckles. I tore across the street to get my playmate, Cliff McHugh. Dickie Bock, the sculptor, squinted his eyes in her direction, then pressed the clay into curves like those she was made of. Papa came to the balcony and scrutinized Dickie's work. All of a sudden he ripped it apart. Dickie watched him with big tears streaming down his cheeks, then proceeded to do the parts over to suit Dad.

Papa spied us, chased us off the roof, brought us in and sat us down next to Dickie. Here we could get the artistic viewpoint. Papa said Dickie was modeling a statue for the Dana house to symbolize Tennyson's immortal lines:

> *Flower in the crannied wall,*
> *I pluck you out of the crannies,*
> *I hold you here, root and all, in my hand,*
> *Little flower—but if I could understand*
> *What you are, root and all, and all in all,*
> *I should know what God and man is.*

We lost interest. Bees buzzed, frogs croaked, we could hear them through the open window. Sap flowed, life hummed— spring was in the air. I wanted but one thing now—to get back to making whistles from the branches of the big willow tree that grew right up through the house and spread its giant limbs over the rooftops.

One day, without previous warning, at least to me, a Cecilian Piano Player was rolled into our house. Papa pushed it up to the keyboard of his Steinway concert grand and pumped Beethoven by the roll. His eyes closed, his head and hands swaying over the throttles, I think he imagined he was Beethoven. He looked like Beethoven, and, with the help of the Cecilian, he played like him. As he went at this thing, his motions suggested revenge for those days when he was compelled to pump his father's organ till he collapsed. It seemed to me that he was now hell-bent on pumping this thing till it collapsed. It did!

Then the complicated procedure began. Instead of sitting on the bench playing the Beethoven, he now sat on the floor and played with the parts. This went on for days. He finally tinkered it together, but it was never the same.

Papa liked vaudeville!

Vaudeville liked Papa!

When in the theater, tam, stick and all, he would parade down the aisle to his seat, pause—swing about toward the audience, remove his cape—look right, left, up into the balconies like a Caesar about to make an oration—then, he would sit down.

His laugh was so contagious it sent the audience into spasms. One night the comedian, laughing all the while himself, looked directly at him and bowed in tribute.

Dad would sit in quiet ecstasy when we would go to the great Auditorium Theater, the work of his master, Louis Sullivan. He told me, then, that the auditorium was acknowledged to be the greatest building achievement of the period, and to this day, all things considered, it is probably the best room for opera yet built in the world. He would point out where his own feeling of flatter planes crept into the detail, eliminating much of the free-flowing efflorescence of Sullivan's leaf ornament. This was conspicuously apparent on the gilded plaster reliefs of the proscenium, inscribed with the names of great composers. He called my attention to Beethoven. "Beethoven is not for the shallow," he said. "Beethoven believed that the barriers are not yet erected which can say to aspiring genius, 'Thus far and no farther.'"

Papa liked to read "Mr. Dooley." Before the reading was over no one knew who was laughing at him or what he read. He would go into convulsions before he gained much headway. I laughed at Papa. I think his favorite was "Life at Newport." Mr. Dooley tells Mr. Hennessy about the "great goin's on at Newport."

"What's Newport?" said Mr. Hennessy.

"I r-read about it ivry day in th' pa-aper," said Mr. Dooley; "an' I know. 'Tis th' socyal capital iv America . . . 'Tis like Wash'nton, on'y it costs more. 'Tis where th' socyal ligislachure meets wanst a year an' decides how long we'll wear our coats this season an' how often, an' how our yachts 'll be cut an' our frinds. 'Tis there th' millyionaire meets his wife that was, an' inthrajooces her to his wife that is to be, if she can break away fr'm her husband that ought n't to've been.

"Yes, sir, it must be th' gran' place. But 'tis no aisy thing livin' there. In th' first place, ye must have th' money an' ye must have th' look iv havin' it, an' ye must look as though it belonged to ye. That last's th' hardest thing iv all. No matther how much coin a man has if it hasn't been siparated fr'm th' man that arned it so long that th' man that has it can go a'round without th' fear iv a mechanic's lien in his eye, they tear up his ticket at th' box-office. Not fr him th' patent midicine dance where th' nobility goes as little liver pills, not fr him th' vigitable party where th' signs iv aristocrasy appears radyantly clad as onions an' egg-plants, not fr him th' jolt fr'm Mrs. Bilcoort or th' quick left fr'm Mrs. Rasther. He's set back to about Cooney Island, an' there he stays till his money stops baggin' at th' knees an' climbin' up over th' collar.

"But 'tis th' millyionaire's dhream to land there. He starts

30

in as foreman in a can facthry. By an' by, he larns that wan iv th' men wurrukin' f'r him has invinted a top ye can spin with a pair iv scissors, an' he throws him down an' takes it away fr'm him. He's a robber, says ye? He is while he's got th' other man down. But whin he gets up, he's a magnate. Thin he sells out his wurruks to a thrust, an' thin he sells out th' thrust to th' thrustful, an' thin he begins his weary march to Newport. First he has a house on Mitchigan Avnoo with ir'n dogs on th' lawn. Thin he builds a palachial mansion at Oconomowoc. They're beginnin' to hear about him now. Thin he moves down to th' seashore an' roughs it with th' Purytans, an' fin'lly he lands. 'Tis a summer's mornin' as his yacht steams slowly up to Newport. Th' aged millyionaire is propped up on th' deck, as th' sunlight sthrikes th' homes iv luxury an' alimony, a smile crosses his face. 'Is that th' house iv Mrs. Rasther?' he says. 'It is,' says th' weepin' family. 'An' is that where Mr. A.E.I.O.U. an' sometimes W. an' Y. Belcoort lives?' 'That's th' house.' 'Thin,' he says, 'put me congress gaiters undher th' bed an' hide me fine-cut where none can see it,' he says. 'I die contint,' he says. . ."

Papa attracted interesting persons to the house that was our home. They would often stay to dinner, sometimes overnight. They did not come with the view of receiving Papa's responsive consolation. He cheated his friends out of sad comfort. If they came downcast, Papa would roguishly laugh them out of it. He was an epic of wit and merriment that gave our home the feeling of a jolly carnival. He had a way of his own of wringing a laugh from tears, and turning frowns into smiles.

The visitor who stands out most vividly in my mind was

Honoré Jackson, a métis, French-Indian. Honoré was right-hand man to Louis Riel who led the Red River rebellion in Canada. Riel was a brilliant, eloquent, magnetic rogue who could outrun Honoré. Riel fled across the border to the United States, but Honoré didn't run fast enough. He was captured and put into prison from which he later escaped and came to the United States. He made soapbox speeches in the cause of labor. He was always promoting some involved occult project. Honoré lived in a room that he portioned off for himself in the rear of a pickle factory and made his furniture from orange crates. I think he originated the Unit System of Furniture. The crates, all the same size, were piled together in a variety of combinations to make bookcases, tables, chairs and a bed. I would visit him in the pickle factory where he made my blood curdle with his wild Indian yarns. Papa didn't take him seriously.

A man named Rabindranath Tagore stopped in from some foreign land. I know now that he came from India, then. A deep mystery surrounded him, an air of profundity was in every swish of his long robes. He had long white hair, a mustache, and a beard that fell on his chest like snow. His country people called him "the Soul of Bengal." When he was a boy his parents sent him into the Himalaya Mountains so that he could learn the wonders of solitude and space. I think that's what made him so quiet.

Mr. Ashbee, a British architect, spoke English rather differently from Papa.

Elbert Hubbard was almost as picturesque as was Father—they talked arts, crafts and philosophy by the hour. Said Elbert the Hubbard to the Papa one night, "Modesty being egotism turned wrong side out, let me say here that I am an orator, a great orator! I have health, gesture, imagination, voice, vocabulary, taste, ideas—I acknowledge it myself. What I lack in shape I make up in nerve. . ." Said Dad the Papa to the Hubbard, "Not only do I intend to be the greatest architect who has yet lived, but the greatest who will ever live. Yes, I intend to be the greatest architect of all time, and I do hereunto affix 'the red square' and sign my name to this warning." Just a couple of boys trying to get along. But Dad's ego is naïve. Said Sennemūt the Pasha, Queen Hatshepsōwet's architect, "I was the greatest of the great in the whole land; one who had audience alone in the Privy Council. I was a real favorite of the king; foreman of the foremen; superior of the great; one to whom the affairs of Egypt were reported. I was a noble who was obeyed. I had access to the writings of the prophets; there was nothing which I did not know concerning what had happened since the beginning. . . ."**

**[JLLW] and long ago said Isaiah

David Thoreau, Walt Whitman, Emerson and Henry Van Dyke were Papa's friends, too. They never flattered him, but I think he liked them best of all. He spent long hours printing selections from their writings on tracing cloth. He would blueprint them and pass them out to his friends.

I have often wondered if his inspiration for Broadacre City* did not come from Walt Whitman's "Song of the Broad Axe":**

**[FLLW] (No, the song came from the same place—that's all)

The place where a great city stands is not the place of stretch'd wharves, docks, manufactures, deposits or produce merely. . . .

*For an illustrated view of Broadacre City see *Architectural Record*, April, 1935—The *Architectural Forum*, January, 1938.

Nor the place of the tallest and costliest buildings . . .
Nor the place of the most numerous population.
Where the city stands that is belov'd . . . no monuments
exist to heroes but in the common words and deeds . . .
Where the slave ceases, and the master of the slave ceases . . .
Where the citizen is always the head and ideal, and the Presi-
dent, Mayor, Governor . . . are agents for pay,
Where children are taught to be laws to themselves, and to
depend on themselves . . .
Where speculations on the soul are encouraged . . .
Where the city of the cleanliness of the sexes stands,
Where the city of the healthiest fathers stands,
Where the city of the best-bodied mothers stands,
There the great city stands.

Papa liked poetry.
One verse painted on the face of the drafting-room balcony
left this lasting impression with me. ". . . And by that light,
now mark my word, we'll build the perfect ship." I remember, too, the verse carved in a wooden panel over the living-
room fireplace: ". . . Around this hearth let no one speak
evil of any man . . ."*

"Skinny" Giannini from Italy painted American Indians in
brilliant colors on the walls of Papa's bedroom. On one wall
was a full-length Indian chief peering out over the plains, one
hand shading his eyes. On the opposite wall, his squaw stood
holding a water jug.
Papa liked Indians!
Maybe he thought of himself every time he looked at the
big chief, for later in life and to this day he stands in much

*[JLLW] and carved in wood beams in his Hillside School
Building, ". . . mount up with wings as eagles" and "comfort ye comfort ye my people saith your God."

34

the same pose on the big stone outcropping of the hilltop overlooking his vast estate.

A young student who visited him put it this way: "The impression I have of Frank Lloyd Wright, is his customary pose on Sunday when the inquisitive roam about Taliesin.* There he stands—tam, cape and stick—like the lord overlooking his domain—the highbrow on a slab of rock on the crest of the 'eyebrow' while the peons move about wondering at the creations of this queer genius."

William Drummond, Francis Berry Byrne, Walter Burley Griffin, Albert McArthur, Marion Mahony, Isabel Roberts and George Willis were the draftsmen. Five men, two women. They wore flowing ties and smocks suitable to the realm. The men wore their hair like Papa, all except Albert, he didn't have enough hair.

They worshiped Papa!
Papa liked them!
I know now that each one of them was then making valuable contributions to the pioneering of the modern American architecture for which my father gets the full glory, headaches and recognition today!**

There was heavy-footed, light-headed, kinky-haired Black Kelly and a cook to match. Kelly was the janitor except when he was currying and polishing Papa's big black horse—which he was doing most of the time. Kelly moved slowly but was loyal; Papa loved the adulation he gave him.

Alma, "not much for beauty but hell for strong," came in to do the laundry and tweak my ear.

**[JLLW] I can hear Dad say,

[FLLW] "(What a shame to rob them so!)" [Editor] Quotation marks inserted by JLLW.

[Editor] These two glosses make sense when one remembers that FLLW wrote his first.

*Taliesin: Frank Lloyd Wright Estate, Spring Green, Wisconsin; literally the Welsh word Taliesin means "shining brow."

The Sheriff used to come around once in a while too. He liked Papa and they would have visits together.

Papa never carried keys. The house that was our home was never locked. At an early hour one morning, a burglar visited us. While he was feeling at home and helping himself, Papa turned on the lights so he could see better. Papa told him he could hurt himself working in the dark and asked him why so handsome a fellow didn't get out and work in the light where he could be seen and appreciated. When they parted,

The burglar liked Papa!

Papa liked the burglar!*

Papa's aunts, Ellen and Jane Lloyd Jones, were the founders of the first co-educational private school in this country*—the Hillside Home School.* Dad designed the buildings for them. He liked the poem they used to guide them in the teaching of children:

> *Voice of the Country-side*
> *I Teach*
> *The earth and soil to them that toil,*
> *The plants that grow, the winds that blow*
> *The streams that run in rain and sun*
> *Throughout the year;*
> *And then I lead through wood and mead*
> *Through mould and sod*
> *Out unto God. With love and cheer*
> *I Teach.*

The relatives were in and out and about, but the seat of government continued unchanged.* They knew Papa couldn't fire them, still they never crossed him—much! The most dis-

*[JLLW] "When they parted, The burglar liked Papa! Papa liked the burglar!" marked for deletion.

*[JLLW] 1887

*[JLLW] their motto "YN ENW DUW A PHOB DAIONI." Translate: see Hillside book. The "Aunts" were among the few that understood their nephew Frank's aspirations and took his architectural fee in tuition for Lloyd and myself. [Editor] The motto in Welsh translates as "In the name of God and all goodness."

*[FLLW] Neither they nor the American Institute of Architects understood much of the significance of Papa's work.

tinguished-looking one was Grandma Wright, Papa's mama, "Sister Anna" to her brothers and sisters.

By this time Papa's papa had left Papa's mama. Papa's mama adored my papa. He settled her in a house next door with her talented daughter, Maginel.

Mama's family came to live in Oak Park, too, including White Grandma, Blue Grandma and Grandpa Sam Tobin. White Grandma was Papa's grandma-in-law; Blue Grandma, Papa's mama-in-law; Grandpa Sam, Papa's papa-in-law. When I gave red-haired Blue Grandma the name that stuck to her, I thought red was blue.

Not unimportant was Papa's little army of children running in, out, up, down and around: Lloyd, John, Catherine, Frances, David, and Robert Llewelyn. Lloyd played the cello and "big boss" too; John played with the violin—and everything else. Catherine sang and sucked her thumb; good-looking David played the flute; Frances played the piano and collected stray animals; baby Llewelyn played the mandolin.

All in all there was something doing every minute, enough to keep Papa from feeling alone. He didn't walk alone nor was he a prophet without honor in his own roost. He was the "Interlocutor" and the two "End Men" in our minstrel show —he was Head Man all the time.

Above the counter at Marshall Field's suspended by a strong leather belt hung a Franco-Prussian sword, a real one, three feet long and shiny. It caught the lights and shot them out again like so many searchlights. But the lights were not all it caught. The world went blank—that sword, the boy must have it. It meant *life* to him.

"You cannot have it, you are not old enough to play with it. You would hurt yourself," the Papa tried to dissuade the John. "Now, be a good boy, come with me and try on the handsome suits." While he talked he briskly made his way in the direction of the elevator.

"I don't want the suits, I want the sword," the demon howled. Several mournful hours passed, during which time the Papa tried to change the John's mind. Finally, in desperation, he made a gesture to shake him. He lowered his head till his lips reached the boy's ear.

"You are obstinate, John, you are making a show of yourself and me." But the tears and wails continued: "I want the sword, I want the sword!"

"Come now," coaxingly. "Papa wants to . . ."

"I want the sword!" the imp broke in, savagely pounding his foot on the floor with every yell. The Papa could stand no more. He was like some musical instrument wound to the last degree and ready to snap, his patients was tried to the limit. He grabbed the boy's hand and off they flew.

The boy took the sword to bed with him that night.

The week before Christmas all the shops and candy stores were bright and gay. Everyone was happy. Papa and Mama would have whisperings together. Papa did at least one thing in the good old-fashioned way. He celebrated Christmas in all of its traditional form.

On Christmas morning we would run eagerly to the play-room fireplace where we had hung our stockings the night before. They were always filled with candy, spiced cakes, cookies made in shapes of little men, and surprise packages done up in quèer disguises. On the floor, under the tree, small gifts were done up in enormous packages. The longer it took for the present to be found, the more Papa laughed and enjoyed it. The day flew by in its festive noise, everyone full of smiles and happy, except sister Catherine who never received all or exactly what she wanted, 'cause when she did, she didn't want it. Cath' could be counted on for a series of lusty wails. With relentless regularity, each Christmas, she would cry and cry till her pretty eyes were a washed-out blue.

One Christmas Eve, 'long about midnight, I was awakened by sounds of laughter and conversation. Santa had come with his big bag. I could hear him dragging it across the floor. I had waited all my life for this. Santa was mysterious, he would come and go and I could never catch a peep at him. This chance would not slip by.

I eased out of bed, tiptoed cautiously down the long, dark corridor leading to the playroom — nightgown flapping against bare heels. I hid in the folds of portieres hanging at the side of the doorway. I could hear snow shovels on the walks and Christmas chimes caroling through the air. With hardly a stir I peeped between the portiere and the wall. A figure moved about. It had on a dressing gown and slippers, not red pants and boots. Its wavy hair was black, not white. It was pushing oranges and nuts into the stockings. Suddenly it turned toward a transplanted fairyland of shimmering lights. The brown eyes twinkled. It laughed. It was *PAA-PA!*

Mother and Aunt Maginel were there too. They handed Papa ice to put on the tree. He arranged the bright trimmings on the ends of the branches. After each operation he would stand back to check the effect, then he'd go to it again and again until it shivered.

He unboxed toys on a big white sheet under the tree, sat on the floor and played with each one before placing it. When he played with the mechanical donkey that jumped up and down I almost dashed in. When he pulled out a monkey that climbed a string, I giggled so loud the jig was up! Out rushed Papa, swooped me up in his arms, whisked me back to bed, told me I had been dreaming. I still like to think it a dream— and good old St. Nick, a reality. And not too long ago Dad said, "I still believe in Santa Claus."

One Christmas Eve, after we no longer believed in Santa Claus, we waited eagerly for Papa's sprightly arrival with presents. Into the house he pushed, a bundle of Oriental rugs under each arm. He dropped them on the living-room floor, bowed to us solemnly. "On this auspicious occasion," he said, "I present you with these rugs." They were our Merry Christmas presents that year! Another year, musical instruments were featured—still another, bicycles. I've often wondered since what Papa received. In those days, I don't remember ever giving him a thing of any or whatever kind.

Every Christmas for many years Dad's charming clients, Mr. and Mrs. E. C. Waller, gave a party for their friends, and all their children. It was held in the beautiful octagonal pavilion Dad designed for them. An all-glass arcade joined the pavilion to the house.

A fifteen-foot Christmas tree, fully trimmed, cornucopias and all, sparkled in the center of the octagon. The sound of sleighbells signaled Santa's arrival with his bag of gifts which were passed out to each person by name. The grownups danced, the children played. Papa was always the life of the party. It seemed that the party was given for him and the other children. It never started till he arrived and it ended when he left. Mrs. Waller was a gracious hostess.

Papa liked Mrs. Waller—Mr. Waller, too!

Mrs. Waller liked Papa—so did Mr. Waller!* Mother always looked pretty at the parties. She wore the dresses Papa designed for her.

Papa designed most of Mama's dresses.

Most of Mama's dresses were brown!

When the Susan Laurence Dana Estate was completed in Springfield, Mrs. Dana threw a housewarming for everyone who had working on the building. It was really a mixed crowd, all formally dressed in owned or rental attire. One of the hod carriers brought his twelve children. Except for the formal getups, it could have been called a democratic affair. Papa was master of ceremonies. He looked like a Three-Tail Pasha among his people. I think the party was given for him.

Papa liked Mrs. Dana!

Mrs. Dana liked Papa!

I liked to smell her *Chanel.* So did Paa-pa.*

Mrs. Dana enjoyed giving beautiful and expensive gifts to her friends. One day she sent a rare collection of brown, black and blue-white diamonds to Mama, by way of Papa. Mama made Papa return them promptly!

Mr. W. E. Martin, the manufacturer of E.Z. stove and shoe polish, was one of Dad's enthusiastic clients, exceedingly interested in his work. At times he would ride with Papa on his supervision trips.

The Avery Coonley estate was one of Papa's most complete

*[JLLW] "Papa like Mrs. Waller—Mr. Waller, too! Mrs. Waller liked Papa—so did Mr. Waller!" marked for deletion.

*[JLLW] "Papa liked Mrs. Dana! Mrs. Dana liked Papa! I liked to smell her Chanel. So did Paa-pa." marked for deletion.

creations. He designed everything in and about the house including table service and linens—even some of Mrs. Coonley's dresses to harmonize with the interiors. Mrs. Coonley liked Papa! Papa liked Mrs. Coonley! One Sunday noon Papa strolled in to inspect some interior finishings. He expected to stay only a few minutes. The Coonleys invited him to dinner. Three hours later Papa remembered Mr. Martin, waiting in the automobile. . . . Mr. Martin was a hardheaded, two-fisted business man . . . but,

Mr. Martin liked Papa!*

He was later instrumental in procuring an important commission for Dad, the Larkin Administration Building in Buffalo, the first commercial building built in America without a classic entablature.

The Winslows, who owned one of Dad's outstanding early creations, often invited us to suppers. Mrs. Winslow was vivacious and pretty. Papa liked Mrs. Winslow! Mrs. Winslow liked Papa! All his clients, like his buildings, had style, snap and were interesting.

During the winter nights of eighteen ninety-six and -seven, Dad and Mr. Winslow worked on the magnificant book, *The House Beautiful*. They printed by hand, on handmade paper, 12 x 14 inches, ninety copies of this matchless book in the basement of Mr. Winslow's River Forest home—then gave them to their friends. Dad designed the setting and drew the intricate pattern freehand with pen and ink. William C. Gannet wrote the text. I am the proud possessor of number fifty-two.

To have put so much thought, energy and time into a work that frames so glorious an exposition on home, speaks clearly

*[JLLW] ". . . but, Mr. Martin liked Papa!" marked for deletion.

of my father's inner feeling in relation to his home and family. So rare a beauty of thought, design and workmanship should have been more widely distributed. I cannot reproduce the book in its own beauty and glory, but on page 151 ff. I give the text and some reproductions to indicate the setting.

Papa was a good dancer! At times he would attend his aunts' dances at Hillside School. The young lady teachers were entranced when he danced with them. He would take them one by one for a whirl. Light on his feet, he looked and danced like Professor Kehl who came out from Madison to give dancing lessons to the students. I didn't like dancing until I saw the fun Papa was having, then I went in for it myself and have loved it ever since. In later years Dad designed a fantastic dancing academy for Professor Kehl.

In the Virginia Reel, Papa was a wow! The older ladies (to me), the younger ones (to him), seemed to swoon whenever he touched them.*

Papa's parties were best of all. He had clambakes, tea parties in his studio, cotillions in the large drafting room; gay affairs about the blazing logs that snapped and crackled in the big fireplace. From week to week, month to month, our home was a round of parties. There were parties somewhere all of the time and everywhere some of the time. Bowls of apples and nuts, great jars of wild flowers were everywhere. Like his ancestors the Druids, he had a great veneration for Nature spirits, gnomes and undines, little creatures of the forests and rivers who lived under lily pads and in houses of moss prayed by waterfalls. And Papa preserved his love for

*[JLLW] "The older ladies (to me), the younger ones (to him), seemed to swoon whenever he touched them." marked for deletion.

43

*[JLLW] [beginning on pg. 43] "And Papa preserved his love for fairies in the midst of a prosaic world." marked for deletion.

fairies in the midst of a prosaic world.* Papa's parties, then, are never-to-be-forgotten memories.

Papa liked music! The Cecilian was not the only thing he could play. His musical father taught him to play the piano and left him the heritage of a deep appreciation for music.

I remember the way he improvised chords and cadenzas. In quiet moods he would improvise soft melodies full of tenderness, soothing, gentle, like quiet waters. Suddenly in complete abandon of all responsibility he would take bold flights in rhythmic vehemence. At such times crescendos of pent-up power poured forth, then a relapse into diminuendos strangely elusive as himself. When sentimental, he played Mendelssohn's touching "Consolation." Its pathos and sweetness still ring through my memory. It seemed to me that music transported him into the mental condition in which he who composed it found himself, and his soul blended with that of the author and transported him from one mood to another. He would take poetic flights into the mystic charm of the most mysterious of tone poets, Franz Schubert. Even now, I can hear him play "Moment Musicale."

Maybe his love for Beethoven was based upon likeness. Beethoven, like himself, refused to be categoried, to have his emotions narrowed down, and again like Dad, Beethoven roamed to freer fields, and from profundity to simple hilarity. Many were the nights when the soft, tender strains of the minuet in G lulled me to sleep.

Each year on June eighth Mother decorated the birthday table with a large bowl of wild roses. They bloomed on that day for him. On this occasion he would play and sing:

Oh where, oh where has my little dog gone?
Oh where, oh where can he be?
With his ears cut short and his tail cut long,
Oh where, oh where can he be?

The Fourth of July was a big day. The snap of firecrackers, boom of torpedoes, smell of smoking punk and Chinese paper gave me the feeling of another world. I shivered with joy at the sweep and glare of skyrockets, the swoop and swoosh of Roman candles, pinwheels shooting off sparks like twinkling bugs in the night. I watched in awe the balloons floating high, their lights like dashing fireflies sweeping along the summer sky; now poised; now balanced like daring rope dancers in mid air.

Dad would not co-operate nor enter into any part of the "noisy celebration." Its destruction, waste, the danger to life, limb and property did not fit in with his ideals. To him, this holiday symbolized the courage of great men fighting for their freedom.

He would hoist our ten- by twelve-foot flag. It waved in glory from sunrise till sunset. He loved the five-pointed white stars on the blue field. He said the red stripes meant to be brave, the white, to be pure, the blue, to be true. He would turn to it and say: "Courage, truth, purity, that is the true idea of freedom for which our flag stands."

December thirtieth, 1903! It had not been long since Llewelyn was born. David was in a typhoid fever crisis. Mother, as usual, was home-bound. Dad bought tickets for

Blue Grandma, Lloyd and me to see *Mr. Bluebeard*, at the Iroquois theater in Chicago.

Lloyd was thirteen, I was eleven. We sat in the third row center on the main floor. The gigantic Christmas extravaganza was going strong. The double octet was singing "In The Pale Moonlight" when balls of cotton on fire dropped on the stage. This was followed by an explosion, then the scenery caught fire.

"Hit it, beat it out, beat it out!" was the cry. There was a hush, the singers halted in their lines, the musicians ceased to play. A murmur of fear ran through the audience. A woman behind me stood up and shrieked *"Fire!"* Cries followed, then the breaking rumbling sound of panic. A strange grotesque figure appeared upon the stage. It wore tights, a loose upper garment, and the face was one-half made up. It was Eddy Foy, the clown, but the only man who kept his head.

"Take my boy Byron, there! Get him out!" he called to a stagehand who seized the boy and out they went.

"Keep quiet!" he shouted facing the audience. "Quiet! Go out in order. Don't get excited! Start an overture," he commanded the orchestra leader, "start anything! For God's sake, play! play! and keep on playing."

The musicians could look straight up and see the Bluebeard scenery ablaze, but they played. Foy continued to urge the frightened people to calm down. One by one the musicians dropped fiddle, horn and other instruments and stole away. Finally the leader and Foy were left alone. Not until brands of fire dropped on them did they flee, just in time to save their lives. We heeded Foy's direction.

46

Blue Grandma was calm and quiet.

"Don't push, don't be afraid.' Her voice was cool and steady. The curtain started to come down. It stopped, swayed as from a heavy wind, buckled near the center and crashed! Men and women jumped from the balcony to the seats below. The big glass chandelier dropped with a mighty crash to the floor.

Grandma took the long hatpins from her hat and held them in one hand high above her head. I looked back at the stage, it was an inferno. Grandma moved calmly, inch by inch toward the door. We moved with her. It seemed in that mad push, some restraint existed in the region where we stood. I was forced beyond Grandma and pinned against a square column. I began to feel faint and suffocated, it was almost impossible for me to stay on my feet. I worked my way around the corner of the column feeling as though I were being cut in two. Suddenly, carried as I had been many times in the strong current of the Wisconsin River, I found myself in the street. The confusion here was as great as inside. I tried to find Blue Grandma and Lloyd. Bodies were being carried from the theater and piled high in wagons and trucks. Seven hundred people lost their lives. My pretty twenty-year-old cousin, Rosalind* Parish, was one of them. She, with a group of Wisconsin college girls, sat in the balcony.

*[JLLW] "Rosalind" changed to "Rosamond"

I stood on the curb, in the cold, looking for Lloyd and Blue Grandma. A group of hatless men wearing smocks were pushing their way from the street toward the theater. I saw PAA-PA! I ran to him. He didn't talk, he just reached out and held me. I told him I had been separated from Grandma and Lloyd in the theater and had not seen them since. He put me in the charge of one of his draftsmen and bolted into the lobby, now dismally dripping with freezing water from fire hoses. It seemed hours before he returned. Then Grandma appeared. She had been at the corner drugstore telephoning and learned that Lloyd borrowed carfare from a man in the street and had gone to her home. She returned to continue the search for me. I shall always remember the expression on Dad's face when he learned that we, all three, were safe and unharmed.

Dad would go on long rides through the country on Kano, his big black, five-gaited, three-year-old saddle horse. Sometimes Kano ran too fast, stopped too suddenly and Papa would keep right on going. But they understood one another, kept at it, each trying to conquer the other.

Kano won first prize at the Chicago Horse Show. Later, Dad won a gold medal from the King of England.

One fine day Papa telephoned from Janesville: "Take the next train, John, and ride a horse home. Her name is Kit and she's all yours. I just bought her and a handsome western saddle and bridle . . . I'll wait here and ride back with you."

Bang! went the receiver. Janesville was the most important destination of my life, Papa, the most wonderful father on earth.

Kit made a hit with Papa when she outran his Kano. Seated on my Kit 'longside Papa on his Kano, we rode away. Kit's former master called, "Be good to her, boy," and waved a moist bandanna.

Kit was a city-born and -bred three-year-old bay from the state of Wisconsin; an undersized horse, an oversized pony

—a white cross on her forehead, white stockings on her legs. She liked to be ridden and driven. She didn't want to be free, she made a slave of me. Later Papa bought me a basket phaeton and patent leather harness. Kit obeyed without whip or bit and had an affectionate way of caressing me with her nose. I loved that horse! She was my pal for seven years.

MerryLegs, the chestnut roan Welsh pony, belonged to sister Frances. Dad bought her from one of his clients. She inherited the stubbornness of the Welsh. Hitched to her two-wheeled cart, she always took the shortest distance between two points. She would cut the corners, bouncing one wheel up, over the curb, then down on the street. Sometimes the occupants followed, sometimes they didn't. This became a game. That cart had strong wheels!

Dad picked Gypsy for Lloyd. She was one in a carload of western broncos at the Chicago Stockyards—a chestnut beauty—unbroken! Papa fell in love with her good looks. That was a mistake!

The local bronco-buster tried to train her with a breaking cart, but Gypsy just missed killing everyone in sight. She was rebellious at any thought of restraint. Every time the saddle or harness went on she'd quiver, then make a new fight, and her free, roving spirit would come out strong. She was a demon when one got on her back or tried to drive her.

The neighbors called her an outlaw. But they were wrong. All Gypsy wanted was her freedom. She had an independent mind and didn't like to be driven or ridden. The last time she broke away was down the cedar block pavement at Forest and Chicago Avenues in Oak Park. Lloyd, walking behind her, holding the reins, was breaking her to a new harness. I walked alongside on the curb. Gypsy had a wild look in her eyes. Suddenly she reared, gave one long frenzied snort, her nostrils flared and off she bolted, leaving Lloyd flat on the pavement. She fell, slid, quivered, hopelessly helpless. Up on her feet she faltered, then dashed on madly, slipped, fell, slid, rolled and quivered again.

Finally she turned and plunged in the direction of the barn, frothing at the mouth, her harness half off now dragged and tangled in her legs. Gypsy was racing too fast to make the turn in the driveway. She leaped between the masonry porte-cochere posts, hitting her left shoulder on the left post, her right shoulder on the right post, landed on her side, rolled over on her back, slid, scrambled to her feet, crashed through the closed door and banged into her stall—a wreck!

Gypsy, like a free-spirited human being, resented the yoke, revolted against a system that drives and rides. I have often wished that in her mad dash she could have found the trail where the perfume of the sage frees the mind from the desire to dominate. For that's where Gypsy belonged.

Excitement ran high. The four-cylinder, "three-seater" Stoddard Dayton sport roadster arrived! It was one of three automobiles in all of Oak Park. Dad had the factory remake their original body according to his design. There were two individual seats in front, one directly centered behind, reached by a step from the rear. The upholstery was brown leather. A cantilever convertible canvas top streamlined from the back to well in front of the dashboard. The trimmings were brass, the body enameled a straw yellow. When the top was down there wasn't anything to hold one in except a rise of about four inches at the side of the seat.

The good citizens of Oak Park called it the Yellow Devil, and not many days passed before the Oak Park police threatened to confiscate it. The speed law was twenty-five miles an hour. The Yellow Devil could go sixty. The factory borrowed it once to run in a race.

Dad took his sister Jenny, a nervous person, for a ride in the back seat. He drove a block after turning a sharp corner before he discovered that he had left Jenny on the grass plot at the corner's curb. Jenny wasn't hurt, but she didn't go riding with Papa any more.

Dad was kept busy paying fines. The day after I had been warned for the last time by the police, my brother Lloyd was exceeding the speed limit—but not much. The police, thinking he was I, locked him up. Lloyd couldn't convince them that they had mistaken him for his brother John. Papa had to leave his work and walk ten blocks to pay one hundred dollars to get Lloyd out of the jailhouse.

I think this car had something to do with Papa's leaving home. I know it added new values to his life, for it was at that time that an attractive young woman fell in love with him, or he with her, or both with each other. They went riding often. I knew it was often because it interfered too many times with my plans to use the car.

One night I swiped the Yellow Devil to take my best girl riding, but ran into a two-foot-wide trench across the road before reaching her house. The front wheels went into and out over the trench, smashing them both, stripping the gears, and cracking my watch.

I sat motionless with grief in the middle of the street for an hour. I loved that car. I walked home to break the news to

Dad. It hurts my feelings even now to think of it. He didn't say one word in reprimand—that made it worse. It cost him three hundred and fifty dollars for repairs.

Papa was a handsome figure in the driver's seat with linen duster, goggles and his wavy hair dancing in the breeze. One night he took his fair companion riding and kept right on going. That was the second great mystery of my life.

Where did this man go, the Papa I now called Dad?

3. SAINT OR FOOL

INTO DAD'S BARREL of creosote stain I once fell, head first. (It was brown!) Papa rushed me to the Doctor. Dr. Luff lived half a block from us.

I fell out of a tree, landed on my head on a cement sidewalk. Papa rushed me to the Doctor.

I fell off the playroom roof. Papa rushed me to the Doctor.

I broke my leg. Papa rushed the Doctor to me.

I listened in on an extension phone and generally annoyed him when he talked to his clients. I poked a hole through the paper above the fret-sawed ceiling grille and dropped things on his head when he walked below. I put his silk hat atop the sprinkler and sat on it—squirted him with the hose from behind the bushes—ruffled his immaculate pompadour—knocked the wooden balls from between the spindles of his specially designed fence, to use for shinny.

Sister Cath' white-enameled the beautiful brown-stained walls and woodwork in her bedroom. (Papa liked brown!) She replaced the simple pongee window hangings with flounced organdy, or was it dotted swiss throw-back bow-back sway-back curtains. Cath' wanted her room to be like her girl friend Mad's Georgian house across the street.

Something like this was going on all the time. Multiply this by six, double it for the things I've omitted and is it to wonder that he left home? Of course, he had the benefit of a sliding scale, from one to six: Lloyd, John, Catherine, David, Frances—Llewelyn was the peak! He left at the peak, quick, overnight—he didn't even say goodbye.

I often wonder now why he didn't leave sooner. Was he saint or fool? I believe that he was directed by a force beyond his control to save his life! It has always been a mystery to me why Mother didn't leave too. Dad's mother, Grandmother Wright, told me often how Grandfather Wright left home.

"You can take your hat and go," she said to him. "And do you know what he did?" she asked, tapping me sharply on the knee with her walking stick. "He walked right over to the hatrack, took his hat, walked politely out the door, and that was the last I ever saw or heard of him." Maybe the technique was hereditary, but in my father's case he was not asked to leave. We all loved him, how could we help it? I think we didn't express it in a way that he could feel—certainly not nearly as graciously as did the one with whom he eloped. Maybe she was one of the good reasons for his premature, or was it delayed, departure!

I remember the humiliation and lonesomeness I felt at Hillside School when I heard the whisperings and read accounts of the first scandal. It produced a curious feeling of emptiness to be suddenly separated from the target that had occupied so much of my time. It took me a long time to get over it, but I never felt blame toward anyone, not even toward myself. I let it go as something I could not understand. I knew I would have to adjust my own life, and I've been doing so ever since.

4. SWEET WILLIAM

AFTER HE LEFT home Dad said he was not suited to be a father—never wanted to be a father—didn't feel right in fatherhood. He didn't say we weren't his children, but referred to us as "their mother's children." Children were not in his reckoning, he said. To hear such talk one might well think that Mother seduced him, and all of a sudden he found himself giving birth to children, wondering all the while what on earth in heaven or in hell was happening to him. When, as a matter of fact, from my observation, he danced about Mother in the evening, like Nijinski in *The Afternoon of a Faun*. He had built a playroom big enough for twenty children in his first house. In this form following the function or function following the form?

Now, I can understand a man's not wanting children and still having one. But he had six, and as if that were not enough to show that he didn't want children, he went out and begat one more. But Papa said he didn't want children!

Don't let that fool you, that's just propaganda. He was pre-eminently a lover of home and family. He loved fatherhood. No one could have stopped him. He just didn't like to take everything that goes with it in our complicated and restless state of society, and children become a double nuisance when a father leaves home. He tried to make himself "Big Bad Bill" to relieve the sentimental pull on his heartstrings.

He has given me a glimpse of the depth of his fatherhood side, just a faint glimpse when he wrote: "Everything personal or otherwise bore down heavily upon me. What I wanted I did not know. I loved my children. I loved my home. A true home is the first ideal of man, and yet, I remember the third week after I left our home in Oak Park the misery that came over me in a little café somewhere in Paris. Caring neither to eat nor drink, I was listening to the orchestra. It had been a long, depressing rainy season, the Seine most of the time over its banks. And it was late at night.

"The cellist picked up his bow and began to play Simonetti's Madrigale. Lloyd had played the simple melody often. I accompanied him on the piano sometimes. The familiar strains gave me one of those moments of anguish when I would have given all that I had lived to be able to live again. The memory drove me out of the café into the dim streets of Paris with such longing and sorrow as a man seldom knows. I wandered about, not knowing where I was going or how long I went, at daylight finding myself facing a glaring signboard—somewhere on the Boulevard St. Michel.

"I remember when all was well at Taliesin, during my first two years of life there. Whenever I would go to Chicago to keep track of my work I would go out to Oak Park after dark to reassure myself that all was going well, too, with the children. I would see the light streaming from open windows and hear their voices—sometimes playing the piano—sometimes singing or calling to each other. All was cozy enough, and I would turn away to town again relieved. I remember:

56

But, I will remember to forget most of what I intended to write."

Neither have the cruel nor the flattering rays of the spotlight paused to play upon this part of him, the part that he remembers to forget, but the part I like to think about the most. Why he himself has ignored or purposely tried to conceal the father in himself I cannot say. Perhaps his emotions were too deep and his remorse too great for that uncontrollable force that led his course zigzag.

For eighteen years he lived the perfect family life. Yet, in the eyes of society, he has not been a good father. But those years with him as my full-time father with his lofty ideals and the twinkle in his eye have been worth more to me than a lifetime would have been with a "society-approved" father. Actually, as my father, I can say without fear of contradiction: "Big Bad Bill" is just "Sweet William."

5. LONESOME

THE YEAR Dad left home I remained at Hillside School through the summer and worked on the farm. I felt alone and on my own. I bought a gramophone. A hand-crank, bell-horn, cylinder type. I bought it outright on time payments from "Hathaway of Spring Green." Hathaway figured the weekly payment to be what I would earn each week. Over the total summer season it came out even, including one record. After playing all of Hathaway's records I picked the ONE. It was "Lonesome":

> *Can't you see I'm lonesome*
>   *lonesome as can be*
> *For I want you only*
> *You're the only one for me*
> *—and you know it*
> *Sometimes, dear, I wonder*
> *Why you stay away*
> *Leaving me so lonesome*
> *—Lonesome night and day.*

Each evening after dinner, caring neither to eat nor drink, I would go to my little room somewhere in the attic. I would put "Lonesome" on the gramophone, playing it again and again till I fell asleep. But something was missing, maybe

58

more records—I did not know. I loved the cows, I loved the horses, I loved my record. A good record is the finest thing a boy could have. And yet . . . the alarm clock banging off at four each morning gave me those moments of anguish, when I would have given all that I had to go back to bed and start life all over again.

The remembered strains of the night before, or was it Aunt Laura, drove me out of the house, into the dim barn with such longing and sorrow as a boy seldom knows. I wandered from cow to cow with my three-legged stool—milking, milking and milking; at daylight finding myself pitching hay somewhere. It was in the hayfield.

It was a long, depressing summer season. The creeks were overflowing their banks most of the time. I worked, played, paid all that I earned for "Lonesome."

It was the end of the summer season—the end of the payments—and the end of the record! But the memory of its strains still gives me such moments of misery that I laugh in order to live. I learned to cover pain with laughter from "Lonesome." I learned to use music for expression from "Lonesome." Later came "Limehouse Blues" . . . "Shine On, Harvest Moon" . . . then "Sweeter than Sugar" . . . then, Beethoven.

I remember in later years when Dad put "Crepe on the Cabin Door" on his Magnavox. The violin obbligato broke in and tore at the heartstrings. We both listened and cried laughing, to keep from crying.

But—I will forget most of the things I am trying to remember.

6. NO ONE SHOULD BE AN ARCHITECT WHO CAN BE ANYTHING ELSE

DAD WENT Phi Delta Theta in college. To keep the precedent of family unity harmonious, I went Delta Kappa Epsilon. After two years of play at the University of Wisconsin, Dad received a letter from the Dean of Letters and Science. As nearly as I can remember, it read: "Your boy, John, is not giving attention to his studies. I advise that it would be a waste of time for him to continue. . . ."

This was no news to Dad. He called college "the four year loaf." He didn't believe in schools, but he sent all his children to them. It was good news for me. Why should I bat my brains out to show the professors what I could memorize of what they had read of what others had said? I wanted to work and see what I could do on my own. The idea of becoming an architect had come to me in a vague sort of way, but Dad did nothing to encourage it. He had a unique philosophy:

No one should be an architect who can be anything else.

He did not suggest my coming into his office, nor did I suggest being taken in. As a matter of fact, at this particular time he was in the throes of many changes in his own life.

60

The open spaces lured me, so I followed the old urge and went to Portland, Oregon.

I soon learned that I had nothing to give Portland and Portland had nothing to give me. I landed in San Diego. Lloyd was planting bushes on the San Diego exposition grounds for Olmstead Bros. Landscape Architects. I tried, but couldn't get what I thought would be a cool job for the summer—watering lawns.

Lloyd could draw posters, so I made the rounds, took orders* and sold them. This got to be an intermittent, temperamental sort of business. Lloyd put things into the posters that surprised the customers. I soon tired of arguing about this and that, and fifty cents one way or the other. I took a job pressing pants—all went well until the third day when the big gas iron burned through a pair of white flannels.

Dead broke, I went to my room to think things out. I explored my memory in vain for remembrance of something I had actually done well.* All I knew from the beginning was how to play,* and I was always getting into trouble. I played with the mouth organ in grammar school, and that made trouble. I played with the violin in high school. At my debut, "Hearts and Flowers—Violin Solo—by John Lloyd Wright" was printed on the program. Starting with a grand flourish on a firm downstroke, my bow kept right on going down, over the front of the stage into the lap of a giggling playmate, who then collapsed with joy. There I stood—Hearts and Flowers and the violin tucked under my chin.

In college I played the mandolin. My foot went through a crate on the improvised stage entrance in the Methodist Church in Menomonie. The tails of my full dress coat flew

*[JLLW] worked Lloyd evenings and Sundays

*[JLLW] "I explored my memory in vain for remembrance of something I had actually done well." marked for deletion.

*[JLLW] and work others

61

over my head, the mandolin flew out of my hand and bounced on the stage. I greeted the audience head bang!

I thought about my job with the paving company in Portland. While I was dreaming I got the materials piled up on the wrong streets. Work or play, everything resulted in catastrophe! What else was there for me to do? For a while, the suffering was excruciating. Then came the dawn! Why not be an architect? That was the life—dances, cotillions, clambakes, picnics and interesting people. Why hadn't I thought of that sooner? I started down the main street of San Diego to be an architect. Bold letters across the top of a store front read: "Pacific Building Company." Drawings of bungalows and a card reading "Draftsman Wanted" were displayed in the window.

"I'm a draftsman from Chicago," I told the man in charge.

"O.K., you're hired." So "a draftsman from Chicago" was the right thing to say. I took off my coat, grabbed a T square and triangle like the ones I had seen in Dad's drafting room, picked up an architect's pencil and went to work on a bungalow.

The Pacific Building Co. completed one of these "dream castles" each and every day. Each and every "dream" sold to the people for a dollar down and their pay. My work was to draw elevations. They were all alike—how could I go wrong? Cobblestones here, cobblestones there, here a stone, there a stone, everywhere a cobblestone. The foundations were cobblestones, the chimneys were cobblestones, the columns were cobblestones, and extra stones thrown in and around at all angles.

I drew cobblestones day after day. One day I got one right

in the center of a window. From then on I was Chief Designer. This business of architecture was a cinch, I really had
a grip on it now. Right then and there I decided to give my
services to the biggest architectural firm in town. Harrison
Albright was the man. He was the architect for J. D. and
A. B. Spreckels, the sugar kings.

"What can I do for you, young man?" Mr. Albright greeted
me.

"I want a job in your office."

"What experience have you had?"

"I'm Chief Designer at the Pacific Building Company."*

"Can you drive a car?" Mr. Albright asked. I saw red, but
thought of the Yellow Devil and beamed: "I certainly can."

"Then you're hired." I drove Mr. Albright about in his
Chalmers Detroit, ran errands, typed letters with one finger
and made miscellaneous sketches. Mr. Albright was a Theos-
ophist. His work was of the Traditional School.

I had not been with him long when screaming headlines
blackened the front page of the San Diego newspapers.
Scandal! Distortions of truth about my father. This time his
bold unmarried status with the woman of his choice, at their
newly completed Taliesin home, provided the theme. The
woman of his choice had received a divorce from her husband, Mr. Cheney. Dad had been denied a divorce by his
wife, my mother—a legal detail he had been unable to hurdle.
"Love Hegira," I remembered "Hegira" from school: the
flight of Mohammed from Mecca. "Love Nest," "Love
Bungalow," and "Free Love" were the headings set in bold
black type.

A sudden pain caught my breath. These outbursts were

*[FLLW] The truth here would have been so much better—
Oh, you are his son eh—well you must have some of that
stuff tucked away in you too—Come in!

[JLLW] No, Dad—you don't come in here. John

63

always a trial to me, but this time it seemed tragic.* What would become of my father's work, and the architectural career I was planning for myself? I went to my room, too sick at heart to eat dinner. I felt cold, numb, and a sinking feeling persisted in the pit of my stomach. Humiliation, fear—emotions too numerous to mention rushed in upon me.

I knew Mr. Albright's position in society would make it undesirable for him to have the slightest scandal connected with his office. "There goes my job," I thought. Would it be better if I did not show up? It was folly to go on with such speculation so I went to bed. Torn between desires to escape and to face the situation, I did not sleep much that night. The fresh, clean morning wind blew away some of the depression. With a "pluck up" to my heart I was on my way to work. I would let nature take its course.

Mr. Albright called me into his office. The newspaper was on his desk but his attitude relieved me at once and I knew that my fears were groundless. He smiled, pointing to the paper. "I hope you haven't let this disturb you too much." As though in afterthought he added: "And, John, don't believe everything you read. If your father were not outstanding in his work he would not be pursued and exploited by publicity. It is possible of course that this notoriety will alienate some of his admirers, but it will also attract those who did not know him before." He pushed the paper aside. "Now forget the whole thing and have breakfast with me." I had entirely recovered from my embarrassment. In those few sentences he had disposed of the matter that weighed so heavily upon me, and dissipated my greatest fear.

We were seated at a table in a cheerful little eating house.

Mr. Albright ordered cereal, fruit, eggs, milk and cinnamon rolls. He laid his hand on my shoulder reassuringly. "Every case of triumph is an example of courage and persistence. Never let an outside circumstance cause you to abandon the thing you hold dear in mind."

I wonder if he knew that my fear of facing him had almost caused me to run away. I wonder if he knew that I hadn't eaten since the noon of yesterday.

From here on he seemed to take a special interest in me. I would drive him to his Orange Ranch in the Imperial Valley, where we passed the week ends. His cabin was a low-ceilinged, large room. Low shelves strewn with copper pots and pewter dishes lined one wall. Bellows, a wood basket and shovel stood at the side of the fireplace. Here we sat in front of the wood-burning fire, sometimes in silence, sometimes we talked far into the night. His philosophy interested me. I remember one time in particular, I had made a mistake in a drawing and took it too seriously. That night he said to me: "One need not be discouraged because he has made a mistake. Mistakes merely show what not to do again. Make your mistakes serve you instead of shackling you."

He took long walks through the orange groves and beyond to a hill where, as I learned, he would meditate. I ate oranges in the grove, gathered fuel, and kept the fire going. When he returned he looked refreshed and at peace with the world.

He had all the luxuries of life, yet he did not seem to attach much importance to them. One evening I asked him if Theosophists had no love for physical things. He answered promptly: "We love the physical things, but we are not slaves to them!" I asked him if he thought it possible for human beings to be in control all the time. "If one would permit his better self to govern fifty-one percent of the time," he smiled, "he would be in control all the time." He had a way of clearing up the most perplexing subjects with a few simple words.

One day a Mrs. M. J. Wood came into the office and asked Mr. Albright to build a modest residence for her. Mr. Albright handled only large, commercial commissions. With Mrs. Wood's permission he turned the job over to me to handle outside office hours.

The contract was signed, the job was mine. All I had to do now was to do it, and I did not know how! But I caught on quickly with Mr. Albright's alert guidance.

"If you're going to do it, do it! Do it then, why don't you do it!" Dad's words hammered at me. The strength of his genius so charged the environment that I had been subjected to all my life that, before I had had an architectural training, I had unconsciously been impregnated with ideas that enabled me to bring a reflection of one of his buildings into being.

Mrs. Wood's house became a John Lloyd Wright version of a Frank Lloyd Wright creation, with something added—something missing. It was different from the other houses in the neighborhood, but Mrs. Wood liked it, and so did I.

Another opportunity came when J. D. Spreckles gave Mr. Albright the commission to build a workingmen's hotel, a philanthropic Spreckles' project. It was to be a block square and three stories high. Mr. Albright asked me to make a design for it. He used the design just as I made it. This gave me a new and more serious enthusiasm.

I felt the urge for an architectural schooling. I did not want to ask Dad to take me into his office for he had not encouraged me toward this end, so I wrote to Otto Wagner, the great Austrian architect who had a school of modern architecture in Vienna. I asked Mr. Wagner if I could serve him as apprentice for a few years in exchange for my room and board. His prompt reply translated was: ". . . Come on . . ."*

I felt I was on the way toward making Dad proud of me, so I wrote to him asking his help to buy the ticket to Vienna. I enclosed photographs of the Wood house and the Workingmen's Hotel. He telegraphed: "Meet me in Los Angeles in two weeks. . . ." He thought his office would be better for me than Otto Wagner's. "I'd like to know what Otto Wagner can do for you that your own father can't do!" This was the way he invited me to work for him.*

When I talked over my plans with Mr. Albright I was relieved to learn that he was glad that the opportunity to work with my father had come to me. "Keep your objective alive," he advised, "think through your own mind! The teaching of no one man can be final. . . ." This unusual man exercised a decided influence upon my character and course.

In his Orchestra Hall office in Chicago, Dad talked to me at length about the hardships and struggles that accompany the working out of any ideal, especially in architecture.

"Where creative effort is involved, there are no trivial circumstances," he said. "The most trivial of them may ruin the whole issue. Eternal vigilance is the only condition of creation in architecture."

He loved his work passionately, was a master in it himself,

*[JLLW] I suppose you would have me tell here of Mr. Wagner's recognition of you as a great architect. Come now, why should I take up space to recite the obvious and thereby stop the flow of the piece and incite everybody to throw his book out the window. John. [Editor] See John Lloyd Wright to Otto Wagner, 30 March 1913, in Anthony Alofsin, *Frank Lloyd Wright, the Lost Years, 1910–1922: A Study of Influence* (Chicago: University of Chicago Press, 1993), 339n.141.

*[FLLW] Again, the truth would be better—the note from Wagner quoted in full—remember it?

and had no tolerance for anyone in the field who did not express mastery.

"You've got to have guts to be an architect!" he shot at me. "People will come to you and tell you what they want, and you will have to give them what they need."

"Don't you take the wants of the client into consideration?" I asked.

"If you consider the house first, you will supply the needs of the client. Wants change from day to day, but a house must embody the needs of those who live in it. The architect must be aware of those needs, the client seldom is. An architect must have the courage to turn away a commission even if he is hungry if his work will not represent his highest ideals. No building has the right to be erected unless it is the working out of some idea, the practical demonstration of some principle at work. Think it over, John; to be an architect is no light matter."

"Light matter . . . !" I could feel the emotion stirring within me that I had when I saw my first house rise out of the ground. I couldn't force myself to stay away from the construction site. I relived the moonlight nights when I sat on the curb across the street and watched the fantastic forms the shadows made on my first building. It was the closest feeling of worship I had ever known. I would look about to see if I were alone. Then I would walk through the structure, over piles of sand and gravel, planks and pipes. I was happy, in love with it, in love with the mass of concrete, lumber and plaster as it shaped itself into a house—a house in which people would live! In the mellowness of the moonlight, watching my first house flowing together in harmony, I knew I wanted to be an

68

architect more than I wanted to be anything else in the world.

"I've thought it over, Dad," I said firmly. "To be an architect is my one ambition! I'll take what goes with it. It means life to me. There's just one thing that worries me—I've had no architectural schooling. How am I to get what I've missed?"

"You haven't missed anything, you don't learn architecture in the schools."

"How, then, am I to learn it?"

"I'll arrange a private course in structural engineering for you while you work. As for the rest, you'll find a way, John, just as you found a way to get into an architect's office, as you found a way to build that little house in Escandido, you'll find a way. You were born an architect! You don't need the schools! You need to work! work! work!" He arose, walked to the drafting board, laid out some work** and left the room.

**[JLLW], picked up his sticks

A few days later he returned. Two volumes held like precious objects were under his arm—*Discourses on Architecture* by E. Viollet-le-Duc, written in 1860. Since our talk he had searched high and low, and finally found them in a New York bookstore. He paid thirty dollars for them.

"Here they are, John." He handed the books to me. "In these volumes you will find all the architectural schooling you will ever need.* What you cannot learn from them, you can learn from me. And John," he said, touching the button of my coat with the end of his cane, "five lines where three are enough is stupidity. Nine pounds where three are sufficient is obesity. To know what to leave out and what to put in, just where and just how—Ah, that is to have been educated

*See page 136 for M. Viollet-le-Duc chapter.

in knowledge of simplicity. If you seek simplicity in the spirit, you shall never fail to find beauty, though all the gods—but One—be against you."

And it was so.

7. A GENIUS AT WORK

DAD'S SPIRIT soared when he received the Midway Gardens commission from Ed Waller—an entertainment center for Chicago, to be built alongside the Midway where the old Sans Souci Amusement Park once stood. It was late in the year 1913. We didn't have much work under construction at the time—just a few residences. Dad commuted between Taliesin and Chicago once or twice each week. I now had charge of his Chicago office in the Orchestra Hall Building and was eager to start on the new project. It was a rush job—we were to have our working drawings ready for contract in thirty days and the construction completed ninety days thereafter.

We talked about it at length when Dad was in town, but I could not start my work until Dad determined the design. When a week rolled by I became worried, thinking that probably he was neglecting his work, but Dad said he was thinking it out and would have it shortly. And he did! One morning he walked into the drafting room, up to my board and rolled a clean sheet of white tracing paper on it.

"Here it is, John."

"Where is it?" I looked at the blank paper, puzzled.

"Watch it come out of this clean white sheet." Dad began to draw. The pencil in his swift, sure hand moved rapidly, firmly, up, down, right, left, slantwise—mostly right and left.

Within an hour, there it was! Low masonry terraces enclosed by promenades, logias, galleries, orchestra shell and winter garden popped right out of the clean white paper. The exact dimensions, details, and ornamentation indicated by an interlocking organism of plans, elevations, sections and small perspective sketches were all on the one sheet! The entire conception as to the design which was to cover a block square was completed. He drew balloons tied to the towers like the ones we played with at home. "There it is," he said. "Now get into it. Get it out!" He laid down his pencil, picked up his stick, gave it a twirl and sashayed out of the door.

The Midway Gardens were phantom gardens to me from the beginning. There I worked and dreamed, ate, slept in the sculptor's shack at times, laughed and later wept.* As the structure took form I recalled the day when I first laid eyes upon the drawing coming out of the clean white sheet. I stood in silent awe before it. I could see it then as it appeared on the opening night—an exotic fantasy. It swarmed with exquisitely gowned women and men in evening attire—a brilliant social affair. I could hear the music of Max Bendix and his hundred-piece orchestra. I could see Pavlova dancing in the open-air pavilion surrounded by balconies, terraces, urns overflowing with flowers. I could see the acrobats like gnomes and fairies running over the many roof levels in between the acts. I could hear the tinkle of iced glasses coming from Vogelsang's Underground Kitchen, mingling with the exclamations of wonderment and delight from the crowd. Later Dad and I sat alone in the Architect's Box, a sculptured phineal at the corner—a needle of light ran up into the sky.

*[JLLW] "laughed and later wept." marked for deletion.

72

This romantic building, like the expression he bore, was the mask of a great inner love.

The Architect's Box

8. OFFICE RENT*

*[FLLW] This Episode could be true—and so, why not? plenty like it were true.

THE SHERIFF was sullen and stubborn. "Nope," he snapped, "you can't make me leave, you can't change my mind. Pay up the fifteen hundred or I'll close the joint."

"Come now, Mr. Bigsby," cajoled Dad in his most persuasive manner, "look at these sketches. Just as soon as I present them to my client I shall have more than enough to pay all back rent at once. They're almost finished," he assured, "it won't be long now."

Bigsby had no imagination. He glanced distrustingly at the Midway Garden sketches rolled out on the desk. There was a peculiar quality in Dad's voice and manner that could win over anyone when he really wanted something. He used it now. It made one feel a desire to help him get what he wanted, even though the one involved didn't want or believe in it himself.

For a moment it looked as though the law would capitulate. Hope sprang within me. Unpleasant visions had flitted before my mind. I saw Dad standing *outside* Orchestra Hall, great heaps of blueprints piled high above him, meeting his clients on the sidewalk. I could hear him say in his most solicitous manner: "Mr. Martin, my offices are no longer adequate. I prefer the wide-open spaces." I was glad this would not happen, not yet anyway. The Bigsby brought me back.

75

"Nope!" he bellowed, rising to his feet. I think his sudden show of anger was augmented by the realization of his own weakness, he had been about to give in and go home. "Nope," he repeated, "I can't leave till I get the money. Pay up or I'll close the door! Sorry, Mr. Wright," now apologetically, "but if I don't do this job I'll get fired." I expected Dad to become angry. The fervor of the sheriff, however, merely made him smile.

"I understand," he answered quietly. "Of course, you must of necessity carry out the orders of your superiors. I should have known you have no authority of your own."

No doubt Dad was debating within himself what he should do. He walked the floor with long strides habitual to him at times when he was engrossed by some powerful thought. His pacing was interrupted by the opening of the waiting-room door. He bowed graciously to the Bigsby, winked at me, then excused himself. He returned in a moment, tossed a roll of sketches to me. "Here, John, take Mr. Bigsby into the drafting room. I'll join you soon." Something in his voice gave me hope. Somehow he always made things come out right. "What's he up to now?" I wondered.

Entertaining the Bigsby was not difficult. I told him my Dad was the greatest architect in the world. "If you don't believe it, look at these drawings." I rolled out the colored sketches before him. He looked at them suspiciously, then wonderingly. From then on he took a friendly interest in everything I said. It was not long before the door of the drafting room swung open and in strode Dad. His handsome head held high, triumph in his eyes, in every gesture, he held out a check for the sheriff's inspection. Ten thousand dollars danced giddily before the startled Bigsby's eyes. It bore the strong signature of William Spaulding. He had come to visit Dad at the right moment, and Dad sold him a rare set of wood-block color prints from his collection. Bigsby's face reddened, his lips quivered, his eyes bulged, he stood speechless.

"To the bank," said Dad, good-naturedly, "then you may return to your boss with the plunder and a good day's adventure." We made our way to the First National Bank. Bigsby, having recovered, shook our hands and wished us luck, fumbling all the while for words to tell us how glad he was.

"John, my boy," said Dad in the tone of a conquering monarch, "let's make the rounds and pay our debts." From place to place we went. It was fun, but a glance from the corner of my eye showed me that an expensive mood was descending upon him. At Marshall Field's he saw a chair that struck his fancy.

"One hundred and twenty-five dollars," read the salesperson from the ticket that dangled from the arm.

"I'll take a dozen, send them up to Taliesin." Next he ordered a dozen Chinese rugs. At Lyon and Healy's he saw a concert grand piano. He caressed its keys with his Beethoven-like fingers, then ordered three. It seemed to me in those days that he would rather have had six grand pianos and hold off the sheriff than one fully paid without the sheriff. Maybe that was because he was a descendant of the Druids, who taught concerning the immortality of the soul. They assumed obligations with full intention to pay, either in this life or the next.

Dad was now into his never-failing credit again. A gong somewhere sounding six times stopped him. Soon we were seated comfortably in the Pompeiian Room of the Congress

Hotel. The dinner Dad ordered was the envy of a gourmet who sat and stared at us. We ate slowly, luxuriously enjoying the music of the famous Pompeiian orchestra. The inner man satisfied, Dad leaned back in his chair—the picture of serene contentment. It had been a perfect day, he had succeeded in plunging himself in debt again and everything was normal once more. He breathed deeply, rose, graciously bowed and swept regally out into the street. I followed. The doorman hailed a cab and into the night we rode.

9. DESOLATION

I TOOK NO PART in Dad's new home life, but that in no way deprived us of a close association in relation to his life and work. There seemed to be an unspoken understanding between us. He never demanded nor even suggested that I show an interest. In fact, he was careful to protect me from any involvement in connection with the unconventional life he was living. This was due to the fact that Mother would not give him the divorce that would allow him to live in a way compatible to society. Mother was adamant in her stand. Is it to wonder that a nature like his would rebel—defiantly break the chains! "You can muffle the drum, and you can loosen the strings of the lyre, but who shall command the skylark not to sing?"*

During Dad's family life with Mother, either he liked everything Mother wanted, or Mother liked everything Dad did. When the break came, Dad didn't like everything Mother wanted, and Mother didn't like everything Dad did.

I am certain Mother has always been true and loyal to her ideals. But these ideals seemed to have for the most part dependence upon others for fulfillment. In a sense, Mother's happy valley was something like that of a Mary who said of her Julius: "We get along swell together, me and Pa, he does

*From *The Prophet*, Kahlil Gibran. Published by Alfred A. Knopf.

everything I want." This may be safe with a Julius, but not so safe with a genius!

Mamah (pronounced Maymah) Borthwick (Mrs. Cheney, when they met) was a cultured, respected and sensitive woman—a bright spot in Oak Park. Her laugh had the same quality as had Dad's, so did her love and her interest in his work. The many contacts in the designing and building of the Cheney house brought about an understanding between their hearts that made them one. Was it, then, an uncontrollable force that uprooted them from their respectable moorings and threw them out into the world together?

Dad built the wonderland called Taliesin for *her*. In this land of beauty they lived together for three years, or was it four. She took charge of the drafting room during his absence and carried on her Latin translations and other writings. I have often wondered if they could not have gone on forever had they not been blinded by the glow of their love so that they saw nothing of the night about them and heard not the rumble of the approaching storm.

Taliesin has been destroyed twice by fire, but each time Dad rebuilt it more beautiful than before. He has never marked the spot of her burial, why need he? Taliesin stands as a monument to her love and beauty. I believe that in it she still lives and loves and breathes inspiration to him.

The first time I went to Taliesin was during the tragedy. Dad needed me then. It was in August of the year 1914, not long after the opening night of the Midway Gardens. There were many details to be completed and we worked as busily as before the opening. Being superintendent of that edifice was a full-time job, so not until my duties in the field were done could I give my time to the polychromatic murals I was to paint on the tavern wall. I was on a scaffolding, a sandwich in one hand—I applied colors on the wall with the other for Dad's approval.

Dad was sitting at a table in the far end of the room, eating his lunch. From this point he watched me. The door opened, the stenographer from the Gardens' office walked in.

"Mr. Wright, you're wanted on the telephone," she said. I was studying my work when he returned and did not turn to look at him. Suddenly all was quiet in the room, a strange unnatural silence, his breathing alone was audible, then a groan. I turned to him, startled. He clung to the table for support, his face ashen. I climbed down hurriedly and ran to his side.

"What's happened, Dad?" It was difficult for him to speak. Finally he whispered in a hollow voice, "John—a taxi."

"What for, Dad, what's happened to you? What's the trouble?" I insisted.

"Taliesin is on fire—Mamah, the children, the students, what if they're hurt? Why did I leave them today. . . ." His voice broke, his lips were parted and pale. I called a cab and helped him into it. We drove to the station and boarded the first train we could get for Spring Green. It was a slow local.

Mr. Cheney was on the train too. I got a compartment and shoved Dad and Mr. Cheney into it to save them from being crushed by reporters who were already crowding in on us. Mr. Cheney was the father of the two little girls who were visiting their mother, his former wife. From the moment he clasped Dad's hand there was a closeness between them, a grief-stricken, mute understanding. From there on the only words I remember hearing uttered between them were when Mr.

81

Cheney took his departure at noon the next day. The remains of his two little girls were in a box he held in one hand.

"Goodbye, Frank, I'm going now." Dad clasped his hand.

"Goodbye, Ed." They stood looking into each other's eyes.

"Goodbye, Frank," Mr. Cheney repeated. There was no strife, no trouble in their voices. In the farewell they spoke as men with a deep grief—a despairing, heart-rending understanding.

I have often tried to erase from my mind the anguish that was in Dad's face in that feebly lighted compartment when he learned the ghastly details from the reporters and heard them shouted from the throats of newsboys along the way: *"Taliesin Burning to the Ground, Seven Slain."* A Barbados Negro had gone mad and committed the crime.

Spring Green at last! The night wind thrashed the smoke-filled countryside. Shadows of men taking on exaggerated proportions in the darkness, running hither and thither—rays from flashlights darted here and there—lanterns swinging in mid-air detached from the bodies who supported them. The kindly blackness of the night saved him in some degree from the morbid curious—ghouls—who swarmed about, waiting as they had been for hours for the train on which he was to arrive. These were the good people of the town whose so-called religion manufactured in the main by their own intelligence caused them to nod their heads significantly, even wisely, as they exchanged glances. But all the while they pushed madly to see how one looks when he suffers. Pharisees—Sadducees—sadists, standing in huddled groups whispering, and the heinous crime laid at the feet of God, who, through a Barbados Negro, demanded the brutal murder of seven of His children.

There were those of the clergy, too, who later from their pulpits used this tragedy as a moral lesson, calling forth endless expositions and quotations. I wonder if their previous criticism and prophecy of evil could have influenced the Barbados, who may have seen the possibilities for future glory for himself as the crime took shape in his warped mind. I wonder how many of the critics do not envy the man who has had courage to love and risk all, while they in their cowardice only yearn and refrain!*

Richard Lloyd Jones met us. When news flashes of the tragedy came over the wires to his *Wisconsin State Journal*, he left for Taliesin immediately. Dad was growing weaker every moment, he was about to collapse. Cousin Richard grabbed him by the coat collar, pounded him on the back, shook him vigorously and thundered: "Stand up, Frank! It couldn't be worse, get hold of yourself!" Some of Richard's rugged strength seemed to flow to him. He recovered himself in some degree, shook himself as though trying to throw off the load that crushed him. Then he walked with us to the station car that sped to the home of an adjoining neighbor. It was there that the charred and axed remains of the victims were taken.

From the window I could see great clouds of smoke curling upward toward the heaven, shrouding the hill upon which Taliesin once stood.

I watched him as he cut down the flowers from her garden and filled the homemade casket with them. I helped him place the plain strong box in the little spring wagon filled

*[JLLW] and while I wonder and ponder the moral lesson given out by those clergy, I also wonder what moral lesson was attached to the Iroquois Fire tragedy that took seven hundred lives.

with flowers too. I watched his great but quiet suffering as he walked alongside the wheels. The little sorrel team pulled the wagon along the road to the family chapel where no people were waiting. I watched him . . . I followed.

The box was lowered, but he neither wept nor prayed. His face bore the expression of one not on earth. It seemed to me that in that moment his soul soared up to God and besought Him to let him join her whom he loved more than all on earth. All nature suddenly grew still, listening to the hush in his heart. The air itself seemed to be afraid to break the silence. I watched him, but he made no sound.

Not until after the burial did I leave his side. He wanted, then, to be alone. As I approached the turn in the road that would take me out of his sight I looked back. There he stood by the side of the open grave, alone in the world, utterly alone, his face lifted, his eyes closed. Was it defeat or defiance that I gazed upon? I strained my eyes, wondered, questioned, but somehow I knew that he'd come through, and went my way. I have never been able to put into words what I saw in him that day. Later I found them:*

> . . . *Defeat, my defeat, my deathless courage,*
> *You and I shall laugh together with the storm,*
> *And together we shall dig graves for all that die in us,*
> *And we shall stand in the sun with a will,*
> *And we shall be dangerous.*

He returned in the deepening twilight to the undestroyed studio workshop where I awaited him. A broad-winged hawk hung in the air, watching the earth. The little green valley was

*From *The Madman*, Kahlil Gibran. Published by Alfred A. Knopf.

filled with blue shadows. Here he walked about the aching desolation of the grounds in silence, looking over what was left. It was then that he decided that I should return to Chicago to work that needed attention. He would stay now—he wanted to be alone.

Memories rushed before me—when I had the fever, he sat by my bedside . . . when I broke my leg, he left all his important work . . . rushed to Hillside School—directed the doctor in setting the bone. He would not leave my side till I was out of danger. Time and again in my childhood he proved his devotion, his dogged insistence to be with me when I needed him. And now, I did not want to go. I did not want to leave him alone.

Maybe he sensed my struggle, for he laid his hand on my shoulder he tried to smile I wish he hadn't.

"Go, John," he said quietly, "I need you there now." So, in respect to his wishes, I left him as the last light of the sun flung itself on the opposite hill.

10. REFLECTION

SOMETHING IN HIM died with her, a something lovable and gentle that I knew and loved in my father. As I reflect now I am convinced that the love that united them was deep, sincere and holy in spite of its illegality—I am convinced that the woman for whom he left home was of noble character.

Through the years they lived their life together Dad was free to express his love and attention to his children. After the tragedy it was not so. Up to that time he lived life fully. After that time he seemed to have no protection domestically whatsoever, reveling in an intoxication of freedom he could never know. He was wide open for anything that might come his way, restless, frustrated. He seemed to be making an effort to live in the varying and shifting scenes of his domestic life, by a self-forcing, so to speak—trying always to make it what he would like to have it through showmanship and penmanship. Only architecturally was he able to hold his own.

The days that followed were ones of great struggle for me. "Why do people fool themselves into believing that marriage can guarantee a home and that law can hold it together? Can one always control his heart? Does one's heart always listen to reason?" I would ask myself. Only the heart can make and hold a home. Only a fool thinks that he can direct the course of love. One who is worthy soon learns that love directs his course. What is it that wants the heart fixed and placed by law or else crucified? Would it have been better for my father to have lived a life that compelled him to lie and pretend what was contrary to his nature? I thank God that when his heart left he was courageous enough to make his home else- where. *

I cannot remember one harsh word between my father and mother until after his heart found a new home. And why then? This is where so-called religion and law came in. They got busy, scandal was created, and everyone, in order to be decent, became angry and hated one another. And why scan- dal? Is "rising" to the heights that is called "falling" in love, a crime?

The law of change to which all things are subject is a law of anguish as well as triumph. It is crucifixion, transition and resurrection all in one.

Pathetic as it is, the love of a man and a woman, like all things else in this world, is subject to the law of change. This law is more powerful than one made by man to govern meth- ods or morals. If two persons go on living together after this change takes place, they could only succeed in making them- selves and each other wicked and hateful.

With this in mind I wonder, if we who were concerned were truly interested in morality, should not we have found where Dad's heart lay and then helped him go there quickly and all be happy about the whole thing? I wonder what would have been the result had we all gotten together to sing:

"Papa has fallen in love again, let's all be merry and gay."

I wonder if that would not have done more toward the making of happiness in the home life that was left to us. At

*[JLLW] "I thank God that when his heart left he was courageous enough to make his home elsewhere." marked for deletion.

least Dad would not have had to peep in windows at night to see his children. He could have come right in and joined in the singing. We would have seen more of him and a closer relationship would have been established forever.

No words, however true they would be, could do justice to the mischief in his eyes, nor to the humor he could pack away in a single gesture or facial expression. It was fun just to have him about. We would not have been deprived of his good company. Everyone concerned would have lived more happily ever after—and best of all—probably—no tragedy!

And the Midway Gardens? Edison L. Wheeler, "naturalistic rock gardener," said to me just the other day, "The closest I came to Frank Lloyd Wright was in the building of the naturalistic pools in the Midway Gardens, after it changed to unsympathetic hands. I think your father is the creator of a typical style of American architecture that will live forever. I have always regarded his work in reverence. I was in a spot, I could have wept. I didn't want to desecrate so exquisite a piece of architecture. To me, the only way I could salve my conscience in the building of the pools was to carry on the horizontal lines. Maybe, I thought, if I did it this way, he wouldn't hate me . . ."

It has been said that the Midway Gardens fell victim to prohibition, lack of imagination—but through whatever cause, the people of Chicago lost a fantasy in which for the first time in the United States of America the forms of three arts, architecture, sculpture and painting, were conceived and determined* by the architect. It became a skating rink, then a dime-a-dance casino—and finally it was razed. An auto wash station

*[JLLW] "determined" changed to "directed"

88

stands in its place.* But the love that created it can never be destroyed.* Today the photographs and plans remain in architectural schools throughout the world.

To me, all that marks the spot is a single white cup and saucer. Dotted around the rim of the saucer and mouth of the cup is a design of square confetti-like vermilion beauty spots. Dad designed it especially for the Gardens—I drew it—Shenango China made it.

I love to drink from its lips.

*[JLLW] Tho the building was built for less than prevailing costs for such construction, the owner lost his investment in the project. The contractor lost money. The architect took part of his fees in bonds and lost that. So stout was it built that the wrecker lost money.

*[JLLW] "destroyed" changed to "lost"

11. MOTHER

WHEN MY FATHER was twenty-one, he married my beautiful mother, whose name was Catherine Lee Clark Tobin. She was the daughter of a home-loving Chicago family of Irish-English descent, whose ancestors landed on Plymouth Rock. Father called her "Kitty." Mother was the gracious mistress of all she surveyed—a full-time mother, a faithful wife, a charming hostess to friends and Dad's clients. Had Mother been able to direct the lives of others at all times—I don't doubt that everything would have been forever beautiful. After eighteen* years of happy family life, the break came, and it seemed as much out of Mother's hands as out of Father's hands.

Of course, I had my feelings in the matter. I seemed to sense then, what I know now to be a truth, that onward-marching souls like my father never turn back. A power within them will not let them, even though at times they should like to do so. They need recognition and sympathetic help in their quest. Then, too—I could vision a more comfortable life for my mother than the wife of a now-skylarking genius. I pled with Mother to give Dad a divorce. I thought that would be best for all concerned, including herself. Then I let it rest with her. Why Mother did not for seventeen years—I don't know.

*"eighteen" changed to "nineteen" [Editor] Emendation only in third copy in Avery Library, author of gloss unknown.

90

MOTHER, photographed by Father*

*[FLLW] Marion Mahoney made this picture—not me. Dad.

Why, then, when not sooner—I don't know. That is her secret. The decision was Mother's.

When the opportunity came for me to work with my father, Mother did not approve. I regarded my mother as the world's greatest mother—my father, the world's greatest architect. Architecture had come to mean life to me. I was twenty-one. Something snapped within me. The decision was mine.

Mother had perseverance. She lived for her children as she saw life for them, still does—all the while trying to protect them from the bumps that are natural, inevitable and best for them. I know Mother derives joy from such thankless martyrdom.

Mother is happy now, in the *then*. God bless her. But I'll get on with Father—this book is about him.

*[FLLW] How about that experiment of yours in making a wife for yourself—in which I indiscretely took a hand. Money and that really resulted in your being fired—Hey? [Editor] See Postscript, pg. 231.

12. HE FIRED ME*

THERE NEVER WAS a dull moment in my work for Dad. Something was doing every minute. The only trouble I ever got into with him was in trying to collect my salary.* That wasn't a trouble, it was an impossibility.

He did not seem to regard money as having a value other than a quick exchange for what he wanted—and couldn't get without it. He carried his paper money crumpled in any pocket—trousers, vest, coat or overcoat. He would have to uncrumple a bill to see its denomination. He never counted his change. He never put his money into interest-bearing investments. He would do the same, he says, if he were to do it all over again. He either paid too much or too little for everything.

Our arrangement called for a definite salary. But the figure meant nothing, as I soon learned. He would take me to Tip-Top Inn, feed us both well. I had access to his clubs, and at times I could even ogle some of my salary out of him—but never the full amount when due. When flush, he would push a twenty-dollar bill in my pocket for spending money.

The first time I talked to him about this irregularity he looked at me with deep reproach, like some injured saint. He then proceeded to figure what I had cost him all during my life, including obstetrics. Whatever the amount was, which I could not comprehend, if I never received salary from him for the rest of my life it would still be too much, and he would be justified in the matter.*

Maybe he spent my salary in what he did for me. I never could tell. But that was not the point and I couldn't seem to make him see that it wasn't. I did not like an arrangement that left me entirely dependent upon his unique handling of economics. I would rather take a good swift kick in the pants than to ask him for money, but at times it was necessary. He seemed to like it that way. When he worked for Adler and Sullivan he received his salary regularly and even collected it in advance. But, that was different.*

He appreciated my work, even complimented me, which was rare for him to do to any draftsman, but paying for it in the coin of the realm seemed to be handled in a department not on earth. My talks became serious; at the close of each he would assure me that "from here on" he would pay me regularly. Then he promptly forgot the whole thing.

I had a deep respect and love for his work. His enthusiasm was imparted to me, and although my salary was important I could not bring myself to make it first. So, on and on went this one and only disagreeable phase of my work with him. It was folly, as I soon learned, to pursue the subject. He had the advantage over me in that he was quick-witted and particularly elusive when I tried to pin him down. He had been utterly spoiled in so far as paying salaries was concerned. Students came to him from all parts of the world, paid their own expenses just for the opportunity of working for him and learning from him.*

When Dad asked me to accompany him to Japan,* I had a

*[FLLW] Money seems to be the real subject of this chapter but—not fair John—not true.

*[FLLW] And what made the difference? Had Adler and Sullivan "raised me."

*[FLLW] Is this true? [Editor] Comment to text beginning "He had the advantage over me . . ."
*[FLLW] Why not say why?

95

heart-to-heart talk with him. I pointed out that irregularities in my salary would not allow me to make plans for the future. At the conclusion he assured me earnestly that I would receive my salary each week without fail. In addition to this, his contract with the Imperial Hotel Company provided for my expenses as his assistant. The opportunity of sailing with him, doing pioneer work in a foreign land, intrigued me and I enthusiastically accepted his offer.

We crossed the Pacific in a luxurious suite of rooms on the *Empress of Russia*, from Vancouver to Yokohama. It was my first ocean trip and I was enjoying it, and myself, immensely. While I was sitting on the sun deck near a portly male and his four companions, Dad sallied forth and came strolling toward us. He wore his black-belted cape, now flowing in the breeze, swung his Malacca cane in military fashion. His special type beret was its turned-up roll rim was perched jauntily atop his head.

"Here comes the Admiral of the Swiss Navy," remarked the portly, red-faced one, who then proceeded to laugh uproariously at his own wit. He was accompanied by a weak general snickering. I was fast becoming accustomed to such wisecracks, yet they still embarrassed me. I think they were the reason that I did not choose to dress like Dad, although I considered his picturesque free-and-easy clothes tops.

We brought a Country Club Overland with us. But the drive from Yokohama to Tokyo soon taught us that the narrow, crowded streets plotted for rickshaws did not lend themselves to comfortable travel in an automobile.

We arrived at the old Imperial Hotel where space was provided for drafting rooms and work. My expenses were taken care of promptly each week, as agreed. But the salary matter was the same old story: When do I get it? I could see that Dad was receiving large amounts of money—had enough for luxuries, enough to indulge himself in the necessities, his beloved works of art, and enough to satisfy his every desire in both his exotic personal and business life.

Perhaps even this would not have materially disturbed me, had I had only myself to care for. But my obligations made no difference to him, nor did the fact that I devoted all my time to his interests and was dependent upon him as a source of support.

The weeks rolled by. I became so engrossed in working out his new theory for earthquake-proof foundations that I forgot to pester him. We set up a rather crude testing apparatus on the ground behind our office. We drilled postholes, poured them full of concrete, and over the head of these concrete pins we built platforms on which sandbags were piled in various weights.

We strung a wire about six inches from the top of the pins and took readings of the settlement as determined by the wire, and made a collection of the data. The temblors occurred three or four times each week. After each temblor our test would show the settlement, if any, that these piles would take under certain loads. From these readings the diameters and lengths of the pins used for the foundation were determined. In this way he compiled the data that he used for the engineering requirements for the building. No data existed in the standard engineering books that could be used as a method of procedure for earthquake-proof construction.

It was serious business, with many hardships and difficulties

*[JLLW] "and made a difficulty in every solution." marked for deletion.

*[JLLW] Concerning the Imperial Hotel [*The Architectural Record*, April 1923], Louis H. Sullivan wrote, ". . . a high act of courage—an utterance of man's free spirit, a personal message to every soul that falters and to every heart that hopes . . . the Imperial Hotel stands unique as the high water mark thus far attained by any modern architect, superbly beautiful it stands—a noble prophecy."

to be overcome. But Dad had a solution for every difficulty and made a difficulty in every solution.* During the time we were doing our experimental work there was a severe quake, whose awful force knocked the brick chimneys off the top of the old hotel. Terror plainly written on their faces, the guests scurried to the lobby in their nightclothes at three in the morning. But the work did not stop until Dad, in the triumph of good sense and uncanny dexterity in circumventing whatever interfered with what he wanted, succeeded in inventing an earthquake-proof foundation. Again he used his wits to master what before was considered fate, unconquerable. And his beloved and romantic cantilever, this time in concrete slabs, became the superstructure of the Imperial Hotel.*

Dad was buying so many works of oriental art that vendors poured in every day and stood in line in the lobby of the hotel from morning until night. It kept him jumping from his stool at the drafting board to examine these antiques as they were presented to him.

Commissions began to come to him from the wealthy Japanese for American additions to their estates and their school buildings. Dad was busy now with many activities in our own country. He would travel back and forth across the Pacific, leaving me in charge of the development of the necessary working drawings.

I felt it my duty to get out of this experience all that it had to teach me, so that in later years I would not regret having missed certain phases of the life of the people on this island of oriental mystery. I leased a typical Japanese house in the midst of pink blossoming cherry trees. It had just been completed in the better residential section of Tokyo. Here I established a cook, housemaid, and a rickshaw man, all for sixty-five dollars a month, which sum included the rent. The servants provided their own food.

I retained my rooms in the hotel where my expenses were paid. It was often necessary for me to stay there through the night because of the work. But the new venture was on my own, which my salary could well cover, that is, if I received my salary.

The experimental engineering data and working drawings for the Imperial Hotel were now substantially completed. A plaster model, the making of which I had supervised, was displayed on a pedestal in the center of the old hotel lobby.

The night was humid and oppressive. I walked the narrow little streets trying to get a breath of air. I was tired, the responsibility was always doubly difficult when Dad was in America. My money was low, it had been a long time between salary payments. My rickshaw man was off on a *sake* drunk—I hailed one in the street to take me to my little house. I would sleep off the depression.

I carried a card issued by the Police Department on which were the printed rates for rickshaw service. When I stepped out at my own gate, I paid the prevailing fare, then walked through the garden gate toward the house. I felt, rather than heard, that I was being followed. I turned to find evil eyes in an ominous face.

"What do you want?" I snapped.

"More money." I examined the card again. He knocked it out of my hand.

"More money," he growled. I was in no mood to be intimidated.

"Nothing doing—go away," I snapped. Then I proceeded into my vestibule and slid the door shut. As I sat on the raised floor of the house proper to take off my shoes, he slid the door open and slunk in—a serious breach of caste. He was threatening and insistent.

"Money, money," he muttered.

"No," I said, "get out!"

He made a deep guttural sound that bore a dangerous resemblance to an angry dog, flew into a fanatical rage, gnashed his teeth and clutched at me. I felt a premonition of disaster. Except for his breechcloth he was naked. His head and body were square. His knotty muscles stood out like ropes. For a moment I hesitated. Should I appease him? Should I run? Should I fight?

I sprang to my feet, jumped quickly to the higher level of the house floor projecting into the vestibule. Quick as a flash he drew a short, double-edged knife from the belt of his breechcloth, lunged at me and tried to grab my leg and stab me. I seized a long brass candlestick that seemed to be waiting there for me and beat him off. He snarled, snapped, moaned, shrieked, jumped into the air and plunged his knife into my left arm. A hot stinging sensation—blood spurted. Mad as hell, I flung the candlestick aside, leapt off the platform catching his body beneath mine. Down we went. I gripped his wrist, gave it a quick twist, his knife slid to the floor. His teeth closed on my bloody arm. His legs and free arm coiled in preparation of a painful jujitsu. With all the strength of my right fist I batted his head against the stone floor—out he went!

Akisan, the servant, aroused and frightened by the noise,

ran out the back door. The unconscious heap under me soon came to life and began weird moaning. I was faint from loss of blood, my left arm numb and useless, when Akisan, trembling and incoherent, returned with a policeman. An excited group had followed them.

The now fully conscious would-be assassin gave up, dragged himself to a corner and cowered. The policeman slapped him alongside the head with the flat of his sword. He had been operating a rickshaw without license. In doing this he had violated the law. But his outrageous infraction of the social custom was an indictable crime. The offender was dragged away, cringing and whining.

I tore off what remained of my bloody shirt. Akisan bathed and bandaged my arm and the series of nips on my wrist. I thanked my guardian angel and went upstairs, dropped on my mat and tried to sleep.

Sometime in the early morning my telephone rang. It was a cable from Dad, requesting me to collect a payment from Viscount Inouye for a residence we were to build for him and his British-educated wife. Inouye was a former ambassador to Great Britain.

I worked all the next day and night to complete the sketches for the layout Dad had left with me, delivered them to the Viscount the next day and collected two thousand dollars on account. After deducting twelve hundred dollars for salary due me, I cabled the remaining eight hundred to Dad.

The next day I received a cable: *"You're fired! Take the next ship home . . ."* Out went the lights! "You selfish, ruthless tyrant," I thought, "to ask you for pay is all right if I don't get it, but sacrilege if I do. And I got it!"

I arranged passage on the Dutch ship *Rembrandt*, one of the smaller vessels. I now had my own expenses to pay and could not afford the luxuries of the no-salary days, at least not until I had established myself—which I had every intention of doing right away quick! I had made up my mind that an independence without luxury would be more suitable to me than luxury with no independence. And strange to say, this decision, or was it discovery, made clear to me how free one can be when he shakes from his mind the hypnotism of luxury. This awakening made me bristle with a new-found self-respect and gave me whatever hope and cheer I could muster up.

To be fired with a snap of his royal fingers after having served sixteen months on a project I wanted to see through was no light lump to swallow. To be fired because I regarded it the natural thing to collect my salary made the lump galling. I turned my thoughts to our landing in San Francisco. I would go first to a little café where I could hear some good American music—the thing I missed most of all in the humid, depressing climate of Tokyo.

Back in the U.S.A. on my own, I felt a lightening of responsibility, but a heavy sadness was within me. I had worked for my father for five years, and now someting was gone forever—I knew it was my service to him. I was heartsick every time I thought of him and I believe the feeling was mutual. Dad was having domestic troubles at the time, maybe I caught him in a bad moment. I felt sorry for him. "Overgrown, undisciplined boy with a genius for architecture, that's what he really is," I thought.

He had sired, hired and fired me, but when I reached Chicago I learned that he had nursed his wrath by writing to Mother, accusing *her* of bringing up a thief. "Confound him," I thought, "the rascal is like a king," and I had exalted that king. But he had periodically swished his royal robes in my face until the time had come when the glamour of the court was no match for the thrill of independence. I understood him too well not to know that this was the challenge he thought would bring me to his office where, struck to the heart with remorse, he could forgive me for everything he had done, and then continue as before. And I—well, I could humor his whims, flatter his ego on all occasions until every vestige of individuality would die in me. The break was too sudden— and the wound still open. *

*[FLLW] John—This malformation will rise to plague you. I took you back because Hayashi asked me to do so. And you can not have forgotten?—The Inouye episode was incidental—not even a principal factor. But here again—leaving out the facts might give substance to truth—It has not done so. But—John-boy your "alibi" in this case amounts to a lie and is discreditable to you. Think it over son! Dad.

13. MR. SULLIVAN*

THERE WAS a great urge within me to visit Mr. Sullivan. I
think it was my lonesomeness to be in close proximity and
work with a master. When I could muster up the courage I
would ask him for a job. I had never met Mr. Sullivan but had
heard Dad speak of him often as his "lieber Meister." Anyone
whom Dad held in such reverence was a great artist, I knew.

I had completed the design for "Lincoln Logs" toy construction blocks. Their success encouraged me, and making
wooden objects became my temporary source of income.
Marshall Field's bought all I could make. I was on my way to
deliver those I had completed when I decided to visit Mr.
Sullivan. With painted birds in hand, I made my way to the
Auditorium Building.

The offices of Louis Sullivan occupied the entire top floor
of the Auditorium Tower, which he had designed. As I entered I saw a man sitting erect at his desk. His proud head
held high, he gazed out into space. The fifty-board drafting
room adjoining was without a single draftsman—no secretary,
no office force, just Louis H. Sullivan—alone. One glance
showed me that he had no work. I would not embarrass him
by asking for a job. What would I say to him? I had always
wanted to produce an attractive ash tray—"I'll ask him to design one for me, he can't do more than refuse."

"Mr. Sullivan." I spoke quietly, not wanting to startle him. He swung about in his chair, his eyes burned like embers. "I'm John Lloyd Wright, son of Frank Lloyd Wright." He seemed pleased, arose, shook my hand.

"Sit down, my boy, I knew you before you knew me. I knew you when you were a baby, I'm glad to see you."

His friendly manner put me at ease and I was soon talking about the ash try and showing him samples of my toys. He seemed genuinely interested, patted me on the shoulder and called me an "enterprising young man." I was not surprised when he agreed to design the ash try. "What do you think it should be like?" he asked.

"You decide that, Mr. Sullivan. Anything you design will be what I want—while we're on the subject of business, what will be your charge?"

He hesitated. "I like that stork very much." He pointed to one mounted on a three-foot stick. It was jigsawed out of flat-wood, colored in a decorative manner, the long line of the head pointing upward. "Yes, I like that stork. How about trading me your design for one of mine?" I was not too immature to see in this man's gesture the meaning of greatness. He asked me to return in a few days at which time the design would be ready.

It was a master stroke. The drawing was full size in pencil on a buff-colored sheet of detail paper—elevation, plan and section. The plan was a pentagon, six inches across. Five symmetrical, spoutlike forms, for holding cigarettes, grew out of the top. The ash pot was circular. The elevation four inches deep allowed a surface for the efflorescent "Sullivanesque" detail which repeated itself symmetrically under each of the five spouts. The sides sloped slightly inward from bottom to top. In the lower right-hand corner of the sheet he wrote: "Designed by Louis H. Sullivan for John Lloyd Wright."— In addition to this, he had placed my stork in a prominent position in his office.

I had no further excuse to stay, so after thanking him I told him I had better be on my way.

"Are you in a hurry, my boy?" he asked. Something in his voice arrested me.

"No sir," I answered.

"Then sit down and talk to me." He drew up a chair. "Tell me about yourself, your work, your ambitions." I obeyed, eager to talk to him, eager to hear any word from him. He listened attentively as I rambled on about my aspirations for perfection in architecture. He sat in silence, eyeing me quizzically. Then he picked up a manuscript which lay on his desk, its pages yellowed with age. In his low, musical voice he read:

"Where is the Perfect State, where man's heart shall be at rest, and his soul at peace, and where he can live with his fellows and not destroy them?

"Seek this State in thine own heart, O man, and when thou hast found it, then shall it exist in all the world."

He laid the manuscript in its place. "There was a time, my boy, when I lived and worked for my beloved art alone, but now I live for no other reason than my love of youth and my knowledge that in youth lies my country's salvation! You, with your talent, your ambition, represent youth to me. Your ideals represent my country's salvation—so I shall talk to you, not just today—will you come to me often?"

In the months that followed I listened. Sometimes he talked of architecture, sometimes about the sublimity of the spirit, depending upon the mood he was in. At times he would vehemently pound the desk with his fist. "A building will show into what depths of spiritual illness a man can fall. . . ." When he was in this frame of mind I would interrupt him. I didn't like these moods, I feared they overtaxed his heart.

He would startle me by changing the subject quickly: "Nothing I say to you can train your mind along architectural lines. My words can influence you, but you are the only one who can do the training. . . . Superiority in a building is like superiority in a human being. A superior man is one who is above doing an inferior thing—a superior building is one which is above inferior lines, forms, methods and materials.

"For every effect there must be a cause. . . . A building is a screen, behind the screen is a man, and that man is the architect. Your buildings will stand for good or for evil, they cannot avoid investigation, and if the building is there, you are there with it, you cannot escape it . . ."

He used simple words, yet their meaning was not always clear, but all fired my imagination alike. Upon my last visit to his office he did not even greet me—he just burst out:

"Power is the spirit of God turned into use by man. . . . Man is a spirit; hence his emotional, his intellectual, his physical need to find union with the Spirit. . . . Man is a moral being with a power of enormous momentum—the *Power to Choose!* When he uses this power he becomes *Man the Creator*. Then *Man the Creator* becomes the genius!

"What does man do with these powers? Therein lies the

fly in the ointment. Does he not use them because he does not know they exist? Is he too intelligent to discover them? Is he too busy? Or does he believe man's powers to be gifts? Does he believe genius to be a gift? . . ." He pulled open his desk drawer and brought forth a little black book.

"The secret of genius is right here." He opened the book and read: "Now we have received, not the spirit of the world [the ordinary spirit, he interpreted] but the spirit which is of God [the spirit of genius, he again explained] that we might know the things that are freely given us . . . !" He closed the book. "Think about these things, young man, then do something about it, for it will profit you little if your thought is sterile and brings forth not something into the light."

The young man never saw Louis Sullivan again, but there was no mistaking that his talks were not directed to the young man alone, but to the youth in whom lay his country's salvation.

In due time I established my own office for the practice of architecture. No assistance, no moral support, not even "best wishes" from Dad. I would read about him in the newspapers and in magazines, and see illustrations of his outstanding work, but that was all.*

I thought deeply of Mr. Sullivan's words. I couldn't help but hook up his idea of ordinary spirit and the spirit of genius with Dad. When I first worked for Dad I observed that he was convinced that a Source existed which, by its very nature, produced ideas in the mind that could be reproduced in the world. The rejection of his art by ignorance did not faze him. He concentrated on the intelligence that accepted it.

*[FLLW] Yes all. And the right thing absolutely in the circumstances—why not recite them? They are good "auto" stuff.

[JLLW] Yes all. John

The ordinary spirit labeled his efforts as "striving for the impossible." But Dad* was no ordinary spirit. In the face of discouragement he was driven on by the urge to bring forth his inner vision. He would focus his attention on his objective, undaunted by criticism, and make his dreams come true. His faculties were always alert. To watch him at work was to watch, not the ordinary spirit, but the spirit of God, turned into use by man.

*[JLLW] changed "Dad" to "Dad's"

And the ash tray? Before I could arrange with the terra cotta concern for its production I became so engrossed in my work that I laid it away, thinking to have it produced at a later date. But it was not to take form, for it was one of my treasures consumed by fire—a fire in which almost all that I owned was destroyed.*

*[JLLW] "in which almost all that I owned was destroyed." changed to "that destroyed most everything I owned and much of what I was."

14. FRANKIE AND JOHNNIE

SEVERAL YEARS LATER the break with Dad was softened. Scandal had broken again! Dad needed my help—that was different.

Dad called her "Miriam." She called him "Frahnk."

Somewhere in Wiener's *Anthology of Russian Literature* there is a line that goes like this: When the crowd, apart from you, has raised up a divinity and with cruel malice watches the movements of your heart; when seeing you afar, they point their fingers (ah, believe me, friends, it is not easy to live an outcast wanderer) at the remnants of better generations, with their ancient virtue in their breast:—we pass like corpses, like shadows, like jesters in the forum! And unobserved a mighty wind will drown us, midst the rippling waves, like worthless chips of once victorious ships.

It was when the crowd apart from him watched with cruel malice the movements of his heart—when he himself felt an outcast, a wanderer, that she introduced herself to him with a "Violets are blue and so are you" note. I remember the bright and sunny noon in the year 1916* when Dad soft-shoed into the drafting room and read her note to me. He thought it wonderful. I thought it terrible. Dad viewed the occasion so lightly, he smiled when the poetess faced him, he winked and the poetess chased him. He had an empty place within him

*[JLLW] "1916" changed to "1915"

and he felt a need to fill it up with something that is a little like love, or was it poetry? But, as the drama developed and the meaning of the poetry became clear to Dad, it was too late.

The Poetess-of-the-note from "Paree," or someplace, wooed, grabbed and bagged him—then dragged, gagged and shagged him. While she was with him, or he with her, or married to him, or he to her, Dad was so dominated, seduced, coerced, chastised, conscripted, overridden, and bashawed that at times he wasn't even any man. I watched this reign of terror from the side lines for eleven years. Maybe Miriam was the victim of a satanic influence that incited and directed her course. I do not know. Enough, sufficient, and suffice it to say, when the climax was reached, the trap was set. Dad danced a sort of ballet russe on wheels in flight across the state line. It was an act of man that someone confused with the Mann Act. Miriam gave chase with a camera. The country gentleman of honorable instincts was then attached to the court—not of St. James. Said he, "She bargained to sell back to me, at a price I could not pay, the 'name' I gave to her, to help her on her way." And thus a private mangle bangle became a public jingle jangle extravaganza bonanza.

While this mish-mash* was being adjudicated, Dad asked me to look after his work until he could become rehabilitated. I left my work, went to his retreat and attempted to do as he wished, but found that his work was so dependent upon his own personal service that there wasn't much I could do for him. Among other things, he had a country residence under construction for Mr. D. D. Martin, the treasurer of the Larkin Company.* There were still some details to be made for the

*[JLLW] "mish-mash" changed to "delicate situation"

*[JLLW] added "Buffalo"

contractor. I wrote to Mr. Martin as Dad requested, telling him that if satisfactory to him I would handle further details until Dad could take up his work again. Mr. Martin's reply, while showing appreciation for my interest and confidence in my ability, said he would rather wait until my father could give his own personal attention to the work. He said he had put up with annoyances, delays and inconveniences ever since he had known my father, which was many years, and he was perfectly willing to continue to put up with them. He would instruct the contractor to stop the operation and await the return of its architect.

This was typical of his relations with his clients. * I think all of his clients loved him and that their desire to have contact with him personally was as great as their desire to have his architectural service. *

The hue and cry of scandal was over. Dad's marriage to my mother had now been dissolved by divorce, the common-law marriage by foul play, the marriage to the poetess by liquidation, and Dad was now in the throes of a third legal marriage to a fourth wife. After his long and devastating fight for freedom he was tied again—"in family" again*—"domesticated" once more—again "the Papa." Everything was normal and I returned to my work.

Some time later Dad wrote to me from Phoenix, Arizona: "Phoenix seems to be the name for me too . . . I am wondering if you could fix your work now so you could spend a couple of months with me out here to help get out the plans and aid in the block experiments I want to make—and for a substantial salary and expenses of course . . . on receipt of this you had better sit down and write to me how it strikes

*[JLLW] "of his relations with his clients." changed to "of the results in my looking after his work."

*[JLLW] "[I think all] of his clients loved him and that their desire to have contact with him personally was as great as their desire to have his architectural service." changed to "I think to all his clients, contact with him personally was as important as his architecture. Life and architecture are one."

*[JLLW] "'in family' again—" marked for deletion.

you. This is a great region for a young man, it is going to be the playground of the United States soon. It is only now being discovered as such. There are only 40,000 people in the state. It is very young and prosperous, the country around L.A. nor the winter climate is to be compared with it—for seven months of the year. For five summer months the lowlands get pretty warm. The mountains are then delightful. You undoubtedly have some work but you might find one to leave it with, Byrne, for instance, and bring prospective works along to be done here. . . . But that is all as you feel it or may happen to be fixed."

I wonder if when Dad wrote, "Phoenix seems to be the name for me too . . .," he was likening himself to the bird of which there is only one of its kind alive at a time; the bird most celebrated of all the symbolic creatures fabricated by the ancient mysteries; the bird who consumes itself with its own fire and then rises in youthful freshness out of its own ashes.

At another time he wrote from Taliesin: "I thought there might be a little real money for you in your five days a week out here and possibly if you could make your details here outside of office hours I might criticize them and even help you a little with them,—since this job is so important to you. But you know best. My children have always known best regarding any matter that concerned themselves and I would not interfere for the world with their own ideas of any project that concerned them.

"As a family we are probably unique. So whenever the spirit moves, come on along out,—get what you can, I will pay you for your time."

The temptation these generous offers presented to me was

difficult to withstand. Yet I knew I must maintain my independence come what may. My appreciation was none the less wholehearted, nor was my desire to join him. I know that both Dad and I have wanted to work together again, but neither of us ever followed through with the things that would make it possible to do so. I think we have too deep an affection for one another.

One evidence of the devotion of this Father in the Architect, appeared in an article he wrote which accompanied photographs of a house I had built. This material was sent to a national magazine. The editor published the photographs but substituted an article, mostly about the famous Dad. Here is the unpublished article just as Dad wrote it.

"Introducing a Son and a House of Wood.

"After some eighteen years of independent application to building houses for people on John Lloyd Wright's part, an architect introduces his son—this John Lloyd Wright by way of a house of wood that John built. The house makes John a 'son' in another sense than filial—as may be seen even by looking at the photographs. And it is high time your mind be disabused of the idea that modern architecture, in the best sense, is modernistic or any other istic—even Wrightistic, specially not too consciously 'artistic.'

"You will see, by way of this house, I think, that good old-fashioned wood as ply-wood, leaves nothing to be desired in the way of the usual synthetic slabs or any chromium-plated pipe. Swift sure lines and clean planes in every way make a better background for living than lace curtains, figured wall-paper, machine-carved furniture and elaborate picture frames. That is the principal thesis of modest modern architecture.

"John, being born into it, grew up in the atmosphere of a genuine modern architecture without thinking very much about it. I don't know if even now he finds it necessary to think very much about it. But here he seems to be feeling pretty near and hitting pretty close to that idea. We prefer to say organic architecture instead of modern architecture and you will notice that the exterior is closely related to the interior and both are directly related to the materials used to make them. Here in proportion and treatment is, without affectation, the new simplicity with a way of its own. The plan of a house is, of course, a matter especially concerning those who live in it in a way of their own.

"For you to appreciate any house it is not necessary for you to consider how well it would serve your own purpose but how well it serves those it was intended to serve and in the circumstances: how well it fits into its environment.

"Always a great handicap to the architect who works in terms of organic architecture lies in this fact that every one looks at any house an architect has done in the light of what he or she (the spectator) would want and not at all in the light of what it was that the possessor of the house desired. To illustrate this let me assure you that of the two hundred or more clients I have built houses for—each thinks his own house my *only* real success and nearly every client discounts what I did for all the others.

"The young people who are living in this house tell me they love it, are proud to live in it and find it simplifies and makes living more satisfying and gracious. I should add,—they are intelligent people.

"Now, I don't really know what good use is to be served

by broadcasting any more pictures of houses built in the spirit
of an organic architecture. For this reason: the organic effort
is always at disadvantage. The depth plane—or third dimension, the plane that relates the structure to the ground and
to life won't photograph. Modernistic buildings being in two
planes mostly—photograph so well that some one recently
printed his doubt as to whether so-called 'modernistic' was
really a system of architecture or only a system of photography. This on actually seeng some modernistic houses in
the flesh after seeing the photographs.

"Nevertheless everyone judges everything by pictures,
which must be one reason why we have Architectural Magazines.

FRANK LLOYD WRIGHT,
Taliesin: Spring Green: Wisconsin:
July 10, 1936"

Dad says, "As a family we are probably unique." But as I
look backward through time I say—as a father he is "unique-
er," for I can think of him through the years as a sentimental
Papa, an affectionate Dad, a magnificent Father and—the
greatest epic that ever happened to architecture.

I can think of him too as Don Quixote, to whom every
windmill was a woman in distress; as Apis, who was conceived
by a bolt of lightning; as Ferdinand, who loved the aroma of
flowers; as Reynard, whose affection at times was no match
for his appetite. I can think of him in his ball game with life
never waiting for a base on balls, knocking pop flys grounders
bunts beeliners home runs, pitching catching batting, all at
one time. I have viewed him from the diamond grandstand

116

and bleachers with varied emotions. Then again, I think of him in his great burst for freedom, jolting against the world at large with actions, at times, of shocking boldness; driving through life in chase of his own ideals, oblivious of the road signs, skidding from shoulder to shoulder, landing upside down in a ditch off the turn in the road; extricating himself— then plunging, leaping, bounding, sliding, falling, rising; taking blow after blow overwhelming and stunning; ditch again, up again, out again, on again, roaring and scoring in his triumphant course.

My impression of my whole life with him is one of comedy, tragedy, the sublime, the ridiculous, and I never knew where one left off and the other began.*

*[FLLW] The man apparently was a sort of clever-confidence-man—winning by sheer dexterity over those of more solid worth and greater attainments—tho not "unique." Many suffered in silence that he might glitter—I know! I know!

15. WHAT WE APPRECIATE
WE OWN

LUXURIES are the necessities of life to Dad, necessities mere things to put up with. He has a fierce, possessive passion for works of oriental art. The soft, mellow texture of rice paper, the patina of bronze are music to his eyes. The forms, lines, and compositions are orchestrations. The vibrations of colors produce solos, concertos, and ensembles for him.

To Dad, the objects are translucent masks, behind which a beautiful siren dances in her phantom ballroom. He is attracted as is a susceptible lover to something he could never reach or touch, yet everlastingly seeks and strives to grasp.

When his keen eye falls upon works of art, a power beyond his control entices, plagues and gives him ecstasy. He collects and gathers them to his bosom with the fervor of a lover embracing his beloved. The inspiration and joy these objects give him seem necessary to his life.

He likes to give things away, too, and gives only those things which he values highly himself. He is magnificent in his giving. But his own personal love for works of the arts with which he parts is so great that whenever he comes upon them he wants to take them back. He does so whenever he can. Many a time I have fought to retain some rare object he gave to me.

118

The Christmas spirit one year, coupled with a little work on my own, separated him from one large Han dynasty bronze.

After the family had left the Oak Park home, Dad used it for headquarters for some work he was doing. Suddenly he abandoned it with instructions to his realtors to sell or rent it.

Shortly thereafter, drawn to the old home and scenes of my childhood, I rummaged about in the pony stable and there I found the Han. It was in a rubbish heap, covered with dust and grime. It had been deposited there by the cleaning woman after Dad moved.

I had always loved that bronze—the lines, proportion, the patina, the butterfly handles, the quiet beauty of it. I was with Dad in the Orient the day he bought it from a Chinese dealer; a truly valuable work of art from the earlier or Western Han dynasty—two thousand years old. Some time later Dad saw it in my home.

"Oh ho, so here it is!" said he. "I'm glad you cared for it. I'll take it home with me."

"Oh, no, let go! It's mine!" said I. "If it were not for me, in the ash can it would be."

The following Christmas, Dad sent each one of his children an oriental screen. That is, each one but me. He sent me a note: "Since you already have the Han, let it be your merry Christmas present this year from Dad."

A cunning* gleam crept into his eye each time he caught sight of it. He would stroke it tenderly, all the while glancing furtively in my direction. He wanted to clutch it and run. But, fortunately for me, the bronze was too heavy. He would shove, drag and shift its position, always working it toward the door. Then he stood back a little distance to see if it ap-

*[FLLW] But the "cunning" lies in the way John rationalizes "the Han"—Yes—but autobiography is inevitably a form of fiction—We'll forgive this because of its <u>humor</u>.

peared to better advantage. The closer its position became in relation to the door, the better he liked it.

Once I came upon him suddenly, he had found a better place for it—outside the door. I shudder now when I think of the close call I had then.

An elaborate collection of Japanese color prints, mellowed by time, graced the walls of his mother's home. In sweeping lines, suavity, composition, in variety of coloring—Indigo, gamboge, fugitive red, the divine violet, ranging in hue from coral white to utter blackness—they were superb. They typified something far different from the Japan of later years. Out of the heart of the common people they represented an attempt to break away from academic tradition and imperialistic hypocrisy. With the exception of bird, flower and landscape, nearly every subject openly depicts or cleverly conceals some travesty of popular myth, some sly hit at the vices or follies of the aristocrats.

Dad seemed to capture in them the rapture of complete satisfaction. Each time he visited his mother's home, he spied an Utamaro, Shunshō, Bunchō or Hiroshige that he had given to her.

"Oh ho," he would exclaim, "I have hunted high and low for this. I shall send you one you will like better." Then he would lift it off the wall.

He did this so often that Grandmother never knew which were hers and which were his. This was true even with his buildings. Often his clients did not know whether the house was really theirs or his.

I can understand what he means by his concept: "What we appreciate we own."

120

The Han*

*[JLLW] Flash—today word came "an Honorary Membership in the International Mark Twain Society was awarded John Lloyd Wright, conferred in public recognition of his contribution to literature in "'My Father Who Is on Earth.'" Thanks Dad? John

16. ARCHITECTONICS

DESIGNERS* LIKE DAD recognize the spiritual source that transcends any earthly formula or logic. That is why their work expresses something in addition, something contrary and often inconsistent with the bare logic of formula.

Louis H. Sullivan gave us the formula "Form follows Function." I believe he meant: form *should* follow function. Frank Lloyd Wright says, "Form and Function are one." I believe he means: form and function *should* be one. However, we must beware of words. These are foolproof formulas which if followed will save a design from failure.* By following them, an architect can see to it that his client doesn't get a cow barn when he wants a garage; a factory when he wants a theater; or an office building when he wants a residence.* Of course, that is of some benefit. But don't think that either Sullivan or Wright followed formula* in an academic sense, or that any great designer could.

Dad instinctively raises the function in his own imagination to a logic not on earth. He shuttles the apparent logical function through the cosmic until it "has a feel" that he loves; then, he forms the function or functions the form down on earth.*

Just say "house" to Dad, if that's what you want. With one eye, he will look you over from head to foot—with the other, your building site. Then he will start to dream, not about the functions as you see them. He will hear the birds sing, he will

*[FLLW] Wherefrom this term in the circumstances?—why don't you say streamliners?

[JLLW] [Designer] in the fine art sense means: "one who produces or creates original works of art . . ." How better could you describe you?—but if you don't like the word I used to define your undefinable qualities, I could use Humdinger[1] or how would you like Hamburger, Humbugger or Bamberger. "Streamliner" is far too limited, But then maybe you are like God—to define him is to defile him. John.

[1][JLLW] Humdinger: "one of striking excellence; a c . . . [illegible]." Webster

[Editor] I consulted several editions of *Webster's Dictionary*; none gives a synonym of "humdinger" beginning with the letter "c." Search in other dictionaries proved to be equally futile.

[JLLW] "Designers" changed to "Great architects"

*[JLLW] "I believe he meant: form should follow function."; "I believe he means: form and function should be one."; and "These are foolproof formulas which if followed will save a design from failure" marked for deletion.

*[JLLW] "or plaster when he wants glass" inserted

*[JLLW] "formula" changed to "words"

*[JLLW] E. Viollet-le-Duc wrote, "Arts which cease to express the want they are intended to satisfy, the nature of

the material employed and the method of fashioning it, cease to have style."

see them nesting in the protective limbs of the trees round about. He will hear the tinkle of the waterfall as it plays its way over and around the rocks, giving life to nature's many forms of plant growth. Ah! He spies a colossal boulder, half buried in the slope toward the mountain stream. You don't know it but that boulder is already sheered flat by some strong stonecutter to become the hearth for a great stone fireplace, marrying the house to the ground. In his mind, the building grows in and out of the friendly earth, over the water, under the sun. He impregnates the material forms with his own romantic nature. He builds a romance about you, who will live in it—and you get the House of Houses, in which everyone lives a better life because of it. It may have a crack, a leak, or both, but you wouldn't trade it for one that didn't.

Or, say "chicken coop," if that's what you want. Of course, you think of a logical house for chickens, but not Dad. He hears the cock crow, the hen cackle. He sees the hen laying eggs. He tastes eggs with ham, eggs with bacon, eggs with sausage—eggs scrambled souffléed boiled fried and poached. He smells the aroma of steaming coffee. He feels the joy of living. Now he is ready to build. He weaves a romance around the gullibility of the chicken and the chicanery of the human being—and you get the Coup of Coops in which every chicken lives a better life on its own plot of ground. You may crack your head or bump your shins on some projecting romanticism, but life will seem richer, the air clearer, the sunshine brighter, the shadows a lighter violet. You will gather the eggs with a dance in your feet and a song in your heart, for your coop will be a work of art, not the cold logical form chasing the cold logical function.

If your neighbor wants a coop just like it, he can't have it. Even Dad couldn't do it again for he is subject to the law of change—the law of organic life. Each of his works is a separate inspiration though the function be the same.

When Dad draws, down on paper goes a graph of his mind concept, and it sings, sparkles, intrigues and enchants. He uses his drawings, not as pictures, but only as diagramatic instructions.

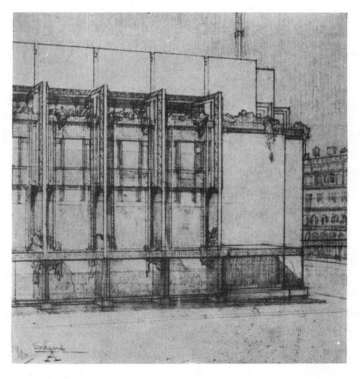

Building for merchandizing. Reproduction of a preliminary sketch by Frank Lloyd Wright made with pencil and his favorite medium, colored crayons.

When Dad builds, he sees things out of the corner of his eye. He never looks straight at them. He loves the quality of the material right out into the light where the sun can play with it, where it responds to his touch, thrills at his glance. He dances around, in and about the site, never on it. While superintending construction I have seen him march in one end of a construction site, poke something here or there with his cane, skim straight through the mass of labor and material never slowing his pace—and keep right on going. And he knows all that goes on, even to the smallest detail. "I don't have to drink a tub of dye to know its color" is his pet expression. I've often thought he had eyes in the back of his head and, like the peacock, a myriad of eyes in his tail feathers.

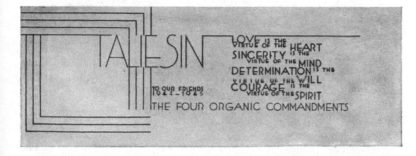

Be it Christmas card or building, it comes out organic architecture—a work of art. Each bears witness to his teaching, "Where creative effort is involved, there are no trivial circumstances."

Bankers wouldn't loan money on Dad's early houses. But in 1904 courageous banker Arthur Heurtley invested eleven thousand dollars in one for himself. Twenty-five years later, when the conventional, "good risk," neighboring houses were obsolete and being wrecked, the Heurtley house sold for fifty thousand dollars. And today, still ahead of its time, it stands in elegant simplicity on Forest Avenue, Oak Park, Illinois, and serves—a tribute to the soundness, worth and practicality of organic architecture.

Most of the complexities in architecture have arisen, I believe, from hooking up organic architecture with Old World architecture and then trying to draw lines to separate them. Why not approach the subject in the first place from a purely *American* viewpoint?

Five thousand years ago, in ancient America, lived the Basketmakers. They used baskets for pots and pans, they lined them with clay for ashes, they used them for carrying water, for storage bins, and even for babies. These baskets were made from yucca plant fibers or wooden splinters coiled and bound together with fiber cords, and represented their entire stock of material possessions. These simple people lived in trees or behind the protecting jut of a rock.

A leader saw that by building a simple structure of branches and trees more protection would be afforded for them and their baskets. Most of them joined together, and for centuries they lived beside their fields in these flimsy huts.

When the huts no longer protected them nor their baskets adequately from the cold winds of winter, another leader, or inventive genius, thought up a new kind of covering. He dug a large hole in the sandy floor of a dry cave and lined it with slabs of stone to make the floor and lower walls of a dwelling. The walls of the hole were carried higher by building them up with layers of large lumps of clay, or with upright poles wattled together with withes and coated inside and out with mud.

Roofs were made by leaning light poles against the walls and covering the spaces between with twigs and bark. When completed, it was practically a cave in the open, yet a strong, substantial room tucked away in the protecting shelter of the cave where it would remain for years undamaged by the elements.

This, then, was organic architecture because it came out of the need and met the need of the people. And yet, some of the Basketmakers preferred their flimsy twig dwellings. Everyone, however, came to see in due time how much better the bark slab construction was than the flimsy brushwood huts. Then these new houses appeared everywhere—in the valley, up on the mesa top, or in a canyon on some slight rise of ground where winter snows melting away would leave them high and dry. In these houses the Basketmakers lived contentedly until some time before the year 500 B.C.

New tribes came to their hunting grounds and fields, and with them new inventive leaders. Soon they began to build one-room slab dwellings in small rectangular clusters of two or three, or large groups of fifty or more—a village all under one roof. There were taunts, jeers and opposition, but the first village was erected. Then the taunters, one by one, crept out of their caves and came to live in the modern slab above the ground.

This, again, was organic architecture—it met the need of

the people and gave them a new sense of dwelling space, light and air.

When war-loving tribesmen swooped down upon these defenseless people, a need arose for dwellings hidden away. Another genius conceived the idea of building houses high up in the steep walls of the canyon cliffs. They dug out rooms from the soft red sandstone or built little houses in natural caves or on narrow ledges. Here they lived in safety and became known to us as the Cliff Dwellers.

This is but a glimpse of the evolution of good, sound architecture. The one phase that stands out brilliantly in this Southwestern American architecture is that the people of one age did not copy the houses of those who lived before them. As new needs developed they developed new forms to meet them. They had no Old World mind-pictures to clutter up their sense of honesty, so following the function with form, and forming the function, was to them the only way. Each and every one of their houses had style.

It is true that we are neither Basketmakers nor Cliff Dwellers. But neither are we *les Louis* nor the Caesars. If we must use forms of another day, why not those which embodied the solid integrity of America rather than a conglomeration of forms gathered from every other spot on the face of the globe? Could it be that we are not truly Americans, that our leanings and longing are for those dead foreign forms of the past? Do we attempt to live on the old bones today because the meat on them provided food for our yesterdays? Inventive genius and opposition did not begin in the Stone Age, nor does it end in our age.

We know that everything new and good has had to fight

for its existence into our recognition. There is always suspicion of whatever is beyond the barriers we have built.

Certainly Dad has had to fight every step of the way to break through these barriers—but he doesn't stand alone in the support of his ideals. Lloyd and I, his sons, "in another sense than filial," and many others who may appear to be his shadows, are in reality reflections of the Light that is his light. These reflections, whether or not they come into the cruelty of glory, are nevertheless carrying on the ideal. We who carry on, live in the wake of him who blazed the trail. It was he who with complete abandon cast off the shackles of tradition and struck out for that which he believed in. Thanks to him, the start was easier for us; thanks to us and those to follow, the ideal will expand and live through eternity.*

*[JLLW] ". . . and by that light, now mark my word, we'll build the perfect ship."

If I were not an architect, knowing what I know, and wanted to build in America, I would seek the service of the nearest* architect imbued with American ideals who has a clear record of religious tolerance, no racial prejudice, no domination by tradition,* "moderne" or modernistic design. And, most important, he must have nothing to do with Chippendale furniture! I would get behind him, insist upon his receiving the full fee for his services promptly as the work proceeded, if not sooner. And I would get a damn good* investment in an American building—and that's what I would want.*

*[JLLW] "of the nearest" changed to "an"

*[JLLW] "modern" inserted

*[JLLW] "damn good" changed to "sound"

*[JLLW] and from my experience the way for an architect to get good clients is to know enough to turn down the bad ones—and for a client.

The column "A Line O' Type or Two" in the Chicago *Tribune* complete disposes of "moderne" in "Rise and Fall of L'Art Moderne":

It happened at an exhibit of 'moderne' art where a group

of clubwomen were being enthralled. The lecturer posed languidly against a background of paintings that ruthlessly exposed nature's mistakes in anatomy, perspective, and color. Beside him was a small table with rubber tired wheels, on which stood a jar containing an armful of peonies and a gallon of cold water. The Jargon continued:

". . . From this central canvas with its post-impressionistic logic of pattern, to the adjacent one with its sense of elemental hauntings, we feel the vibrations of an instinctive artist dominating what may be called the argument of the picture. We also sense an insistent response to the essential form which underlies the mere outward surface of nature, and there we witness this superb artist triumphing over superficial crudities and achieving the Grail of his inward searchings—"

The speaker paused to let this revelation sink in; with studied grace he leaned against the extended table leaf. Instantly that frail support flopped over and the jargonist collapsed on the floor under a deluge of peonies and cold water. For a moment there was a stunned silence, then sanity returned in an explosive gale of hilarity. The lecture remains unfinished business.

Ever since its inception the name "modernistic" has been repulsive to the creative artist because of its misuse. Works of art together with their imitations and impure trashy productions are included under this heading. When Dad's poetic translations, as well as his higher self, went into the structures that were inextricably linked with those that were called "modernistic," he snatched his holy child from the hands of Herod's men and clothed it with "organic."* His efforts under this banner have resulted in worship, argument, joy, hate,

*[FLLW] Good stuff. [Editor] In original, written next to bracket beginning at "Ever since its inception . . ."

133

comedy, tragedy, and at least one broken nose. It should not be necessary for one to fight in order to maintain his principles. Yet a good fight now and then allows us to catch glimpses of a brighter day through the thick curtain of tradition.

These glimpses have shown me that organic architecture is honest—it does not lie about anything (therein lies its beneficence when we seek truth; its impudence when we practice hypocrisy). A material used represents itself and no other. Nothing appears to be what it is not. If a material looks like brick, it is brick. If a wall surface looks like tile, it is tile. If a panel looks like wood, it is wood. An asbestos shingle moulded to imitate wood grain is not organic architecture. A wooden surface whose grain and quality is covered with paint is not organic architecture. A steel desk grained to represent wood is not organic architecture.

An example of detail in organic design is found in Frank Lloyd Wright's wall-hung watercloset.* He found a way to cantilever the bowl from the cast-iron soil pipe in the wall behind. The underside of the bowl was then clear of the floor for better sanitation. Every time I see a porter swinging his mop under one of these closets, I wonder why Dad didn't patent the idea. He would not patent any of his many inventions.*

A word, at least, is due the unsung heroes. The monklike I. J. Gill of San Diego, California, is one. He, like Dad, was a courageous creator. If you knew Gill, you knew his buildings—if you knew his buildings, you knew Gill. Unlike Dad, he shied from publicity, almost to the point of making himself a hermit.* I had the privilege of living in one of his houses.

*[JLLW] First used for the Larkin Administration Building, Buffalo, 1903. Now universally used for public buildings and lately for residences.

*[FLLW] Fair enough [Editor] written next to bracket around paragraph beginning at "An example . . ."

*[FLLW] And you did not know that Gill worked for "Dad" at Adler and Sullivan's! He let his hair grow long, affected the "tie," and was reprimanded by Dad who advised him to get his hair cut and cut the pose too? His conceit was enormous—too? You didn't know him at all.

[JLLW] Shame on you Dad, for letting Irving to cut his hair and ridiculing his tie. Did you also tell him never to marry?—Shame. John

Few persons know or ever will know of I. J. Gill, Architect; nevertheless, he contributed an important[1] part to the development of style in architecture for America.[2]

Dad has a drive that has always allowed him to make contacts with people and fight for his ideals. His salesmanship is the best, because he believes that what he has to give is the best. He supplies a[3] romance with his drive that intrigues people, whether or not they are ready for him.[4]

Gill wasn't so certain that the people[5] were ready to accept truth in architecture, and he would not fight. Neither would he sell his services to those who wanted traditional building. His extremely[6] sensitive nature was without a protective crust.[7] So, he built only the few buildings for those who sought him out locally.[8]

There are other American[9] architects who have tuned in to the same vital Source as has Dad—who are just as[10] profound, and as[11] capable, but who lack the human drive down here on earth. Although we do not hear of them, they leave a light behind them.[12]

But no matter how good were the works of the past, it is reasonable to believe that we should do things better today, for we have inherited the skill, the technique, the art, the talents and all the labor of the past. If we have the right to a higher and nobler civilization than ever before, then our buildings should be better than the good ones of the past. Out of the present need for living must come the forms we use. When truth is no longer a "word" but is *the life we are living*, it will be exemplified in the buildings we erect.[13]

[1] [JLLW] "an important" changed to "a"

[2] [FLLW] Just what? Would like to know.

[3] [JLLW] "a" changed to "an architectural"

[4] [JLLW] "whether or not they are ready for him." changed to "their building becomes an event."

[FLLW] This is pretty nasty if true—and sounds to me like Irving himself.

[FLLW] "?" [Editor] written next to bracket around paragraph beginning at "Dad has . . ."

[5] [JLLW] "wasn't so certain that the people were" changed to "found that most were not"

[6] [JLLW] "extremely" marked for deletion

[7] [FLLW] all crust

[8] [FLLW] Not a fine <u>advertiser</u> like poor Dad?

[JLLW] His buildings like his life lacked national color.

[9] [JLLW] "American" marked for deletion

[10] [JLLW] "just as" marked for deletion

[11] "as" marked for deletion

[12] [FLLW] Whose light? And what light? Be specific.

[JLLW] I can hear Dad say, "Whose light? and what light? Be specific." And I would say, "Your light—from the same place—that's all."

And Dad's clients?—Ah, there is a people without whom this book would not have been written. Each one is worthy (sic) a monograph.

[JLLW] Your light, Dad, from the same place—that's all. John.

[13] [FLLW] Thanks—son! [Editor] Written next to a line drawn encompassing the last two sentences of this paragraph beginning with "Out of . . ."

17. M. VIOLLET-LE-DUC*

VIOLLET-LE-DUC was a teacher of what Dad now calls *organic architecture* as early as 1860. His influence upon my father was marked. Dad, with his uncanny genius in architecture, is not a good teacher. He was aware of this when he gave me the *Discourses on Architecture*. Dad has always told his students that they could learn from his school but that he could not teach them anything. But I can see now that his teaching, even though apparently without method, had a very definite one. He taught me not to say "Old Antique" by laughing at me when I said it. I had to analyze the phrase myself before I knew why he laughed.

Viollet-le-Duc covered the subject of architecture so thoroughly that there were few words Dad could add. So he gave me those volumes to speak for him. They are long since out of print and not readily available to any reader. But of the writings of E. Viollet-le-Duc my father said: "In these volumes you will find all the architectural schooling you will ever need." For these two reasons—their inaccessibility and their basic place in my father's philosophy of life and work —I am here reproducing for the interested reader the following extracts.

Because of the earnest solicitations of my friends and brother-architects, I determined upon opening a studio for

136

*pupils and delivering a course of lectures on architecture.
. . . In my simplicity I did not take into consideration the
enmity and opposition to my teachings by certain Professors
of the École des beaux-arts. The Professors in power, deeply
versed in the study of Greek antiquities—Professors of Archae-
ology, were particularly displeased that I drew attention to
an art foreign to their studies, and branded the teachings as
'dangerous dogma.' My friends rose in arms, came to my defense; but I simply said: Now tumult is the foe to study; and
I love study and detest tumult. I allowed the storm to blow
over; which, meeting no resistance, spent its rage in vain . . .
I put the manuscript of my lectures back into my portfolio
and gave my mind to other matters. And now I am perfectly
willing to leave the professional chair to those who occupy it
with an ability to which I do not aspire, and an authority which
is indisputable. Our art gains nothing by these fruitless strifes
which turn upon words rather than things; while by engaging
in them artists lose a little of that good sense which is so
needful to us all. But there are eternal principles which it is
the duty of each of us to exalt above the passions of the
schools that are so unworthy to occupy the attention of sincere
and earnest men.*

*Renouncing the honors of a chair which I foresaw would
only prove an arena for controversies I have resolved to offer
my friends, my fellow-architects, my pupils, and my provincial
and foreign correspondents, whose sympathy and encouragement are to me such a valuable support, these Lectures on
Architecture . . . my chief object is truth, and if I am liable
to any accusation, it is that of not belonging to any school. It
is true, that alone is enough to array them all against me. . . .*

The more civilized and regular society becomes, the more is the artist compelled to analyse and dissect the passions, manners and tastes, — to revert to first principles. Hence it is more difficult to be an artist in times like our own, than among rude, unrefined people who openly display their good or evil passions. In primitive epochs, style imposed itself on the artist; now, the artist has to acquire style . . . If a form is not the immediate expression of a requirement of a certain social condition it is bad form in which there is no style. To imitate in stone a structure of wood is to deviate from truth in expression . . .

But what is style? I'm not speaking now of style as applied to the classification of arts by periods, but of style as inherent in the arts of all times; and to make myself better understood, I remark that independently of the style of the writer in each language, there is a style which belongs to all languages, because it belongs to humanity. This style is inspiration; but it is inspiration subjected to the laws of reason, — inspiration invested with the distinction peculiar to every work produced by a genuine feeling rigorously analysed by reason before being expressed.

. . . There are periods which have their style, but in which style is wanting. Such, for instance, is the Roman period under the last Emperors of the West. There is a Louis XIV. style, a Louis XV. style, and some have lately discovered even a Louis XVI. style. Nevertheless, one of the characteristics of Architectural Art at the close of the seventeenth and during the eighteenth century is the absence of style. "Terms should be defined," says Voltaire; and Voltaire is often right. Style

proper and style as an archaeological indication are two widely different things.

Style consists in a marked distinction of form; it is one of the essential elements of beauty, but does not of itself alone constitute beauty. Civilisation dulls those instincts of man which lead him to introduce style into his works, but it does not destroy them. These instincts come into play involuntarily. In a certain assembly you remark one person in particular. This person may not possess any of those striking characteristics which constitute beauty; the features may not be regular; yet attracted by a mysterious influence, your gaze continually reverts to the individual in question.

However unaccustomed to such observation you succeed in explaining to yourself the reasons which impel you to satisfy that instinctive attraction. The first thing that strikes you is a marked line,—a harmony between the frame and the muscles; it is an ensemble in some cases irregular, but which excites in you sympathy or antipathy. Your attention is engaged by a contour, by certain forms of the bones which are covered with muscles in harmony with those forms, the manner in which the hair grows on the brow, the junction of the limbs with the body, the concordance between the gestures and the thought; you have soon arrived at settled ideas as to habits, taste, and character of that person. Though seen for the first time, a stranger to whom you have never spoken, you build up a whole romance on the individual in question. Of animated beings only those who have style possess this mysterious power of attraction.

Individuals of the human race are so often spoiled by an artificial education, and by moral and physical infirmities, that it is rare to find one of them possessing style; the brutes, on the contrary, all exhibit this harmony—this perfect conformity between the outward form and the instinct—the breath which animates them. Hence, we may say that the brutes have style,—from the insect to the noblest of the quadrupeds. Their gestures are always true; their movements always plainly indicate a want or a definite purpose, a desire or a fear. Brutes are never affected, artificial or vulgar; whether beautiful or ugly they possess style because they have only simple feelings and seek their ends by simple and direct means. Man,—especially civilized man,—being a very complicated animal and altered in character by an education which teaches him to resist his instincts, must make a retrospective effort,—shall I say,—to acquire style.

In the present day we are no longer familiar with those simple and true ideals which lead artists to invest their conceptions with style; I think it necessary, therefore, to define the constituent elements of style, and in so doing, carefully to avoid equivocal terms, and those meaningless phrases which are repeated with the profound respect that is professed by most people for what is incomprehensible. Ideas must be presented in a palpable form,—a definite embodiment,—if we would communicate them.

Clearly, to understand what style as regards form is we must consider form in its simplest expressions. Let us therefore take one of the primitive arts,—one of the earliest practised among all nations, because it is among the first needed,—the art of the coppersmith, for example. We take the art at the time when man discovered that by beating a sheet of copper in a particular way he could so model it as to give it the form of a vessel.

He can, by beating the sheet of copper, cause it to return on itself, and of a plane surface make a hollow body. He leaves a flat circular bottom to his vessel so that it may stand firm when full. To hinder the liquid from spilling when the vessel is shaken, he contracts its upper orifice, and then widens it out suddenly at the edge, to facilitate pouring out the liquid; the most natural form, therefore—that determined by the mode of fabrication.

There must be a means of holding the vessel; the workman therefore attaches handles with rivets. But as the vessel must be inverted when empty, and has to be drained dry, he makes the handles so that they shall not stand above the level of the top of the vessel. Thus fashioned by methods suggested in the fabrication, this vessel has style: first, because it exactly indicates its purpose; second, because it is fashioned in accordance with the material employed and the means of fabrication suited to this material; third, because the form obtained is suitable to the material of which this utensil is made, and the use for which it is intended. This vessel has style because human reason indicates exactly the form suitable to it.

The coppersmiths themselves, in their desire to do better than their predecessors, deviate from the line of the true and the good. We find therefore a second coppersmith who wishes to alter the form of the primitive vessel in order to attract purchasers by the distinction of novelty; he gives a few extra blows of the hammer and rounds the body of the vessel which had hitherto been regarded as perfect. The form is, in fact, new and all the town wish to have vessels made by the second coppersmith.

A third coppersmith, perceiving that the fellow-townsmen are taken with the rounding of the base, goes still further and makes a third vessel, which is still more popular. This last workman, having lost sight of the principle, bids adieu to reason and follows caprice alone; he increases the length of his handles, and advertises them as of the newest taste. This vessel cannot be placed upside down to be drained without endangering the shape of these handles; but every one praises it, and the third coppersmith is credited with having wonderfully improved his art, while in reality he has only deprived a form of its proper style, and produced an unsightly and relatively inconvenient article.

This history is typical of that of the style in all the arts. Arts which cease to express the want they are intended to satisfy, the nature of the material employed, and the method of fashioning it, cease to have style.

If a Roman matron of the period of the Republic were to appear in a drawing-room filled with ladies dressed in hooped skirts, with powdered hair and a superstructure of plumes or flowers, the Roman lady would present a singular figure; but it is none-the-less certain that her dress would have style, while those of the ladies in hooped skirts would be in 'the style of the period' but would not possess style. Here then we have, I think, an intelligible starting-point for appreciation of style.

Are we then to suppose that style is inherent in one form alone and that women, for instance, if they wish their dress to have style must dress themselves like the mother of the Gracchi? Certainly not. The satin and the woollen dress may both have style; but on the condition that the shape of neither is at variance with the forms of the body; that it does not ri-

diculously exaggerate the former nor hamper the movements of the latter; and that the cut of the dresses in each shows a due regard to the special qualities of the material. Nature invariably exhibits style in her productions because however diversified they may be they are always subject to laws—to immutable principles. The leaf of a shrub, a flower, an insect—all have style; because they grow, are developed, and maintain their existence according to laws essentially logical. We can subtract nothing from a flower, for each part of its organism expresses a function by taking the form which is appropriate to that function.

Style resides solely in the true and marked expression of a principle and not in an immutable form; *consequently, as nothing exists except in virtue of a principle, there may be style in everything. . . .*

They tell you in the schools that Greek art has the impress of style; that that style is pure,—complete, namely, and without alloy; copy the Greek form therefore if you wish your art to have style. As well might it be said:—The tiger or the cat has style; disguise yourself therefore as a tiger or a cat if you would lay claim to style. Instead of this it should be explained why the cat and the tiger, the flower and the insect, have style, and the instruction should run thus:—Proceed as nature does in her works, and you will be able to invest with style all that your brain conceives. True, this is not easy amidst a complicated civilisation, . . . but it is not impossible.

. . . Among primitive peoples the mind of the artist can produce nothing but works possessing style, because this mind or imagination proceeds nearly in the same way as nature. A

want or a desire manifests itself, and man employs the most direct means of satisfying it . . .

The poet or writer of the present day—without forgetting the great authors of the past—soon becomes conscious that he should express his ideas not by a slavish adherence to the forms or terms employed by those authors, but by proceeding as they did. Instruction aids the writer of real merit, without fettering his genius, because the judgment of the public serves him as a guide. But in Architectural Art this touchstone of common sense is wanting. Architecture offers the same aspect to the public as a book does to those who cannot read. They can admire the binding and the typography, but that is all. The book may contain the grossest absurdities, but that is of the slightest possible concern to him who is unable to decipher its characters. . . .

We erect public buildings which are devoid of style because we insist on allying forms derived from traditions with requirements which are not in harmony with those traditions.

There is no style but that which is appropriate to the object. A sailing-vessel has style; but a steamer made to conceal its motive power and looking like a sailing-vessel will have none; a gun has style, but a gun made to resemble a crossbow will have none. Now we architects have for a long time been making guns while endeavouring to give them as much as possible the appearance of crossbows. And there are persons of intelligence who maintain that if we abandon the form of the crossbow we are barbarians,—that Art is lost,—that nothing is left for us but to hide our heads in shame.

But I shall leave metaphors and confine myself to following the Architect through the first part of his labour, up to the

144

*point when in order to continue to invest his work with style,
it no longer suffices him to have definite, well-arranged ideas,
and to know how to express them clearly.*

*Here is a piece of masonry of the best Roman period . . .
it is the wall of the circular cella of the temple of Vesta, on the
banks of the Tiber. The columns of this temple are monostyles
of marble, and the wall of the cella is faced externally with the
same material; but at that time marble was too scarce a material to be lavishly used. The wall is therefore composed of al-
ternate thin course of marble and a facing, likewise of marble,
with a backing—for economy's sake—of blocks of calcareous
local stone—travertine. All these pieces are bonded together
with iron cramps. On the inside these courses of travertine
were coated with painted stucco. Here then we have a wall,—
a simple wall whose construction possesses style. These alter-
nate thin courses, serving as bonds for the facing, these sinkings which plainly mark the shape of each piece,—which
indicate the method employed,—form without effort a decora-
tion full of style because the eye readily comprehends the
strong and rational structure it expresses.*

*Pleased with the firm and elegant appearance of this simple
wall face, our architect on his return to Paris is desirous of reproducing it. But he builds with stone, not with marble; he is
supplied from the quarry with courses of equal height and of
one or two yards in length. Will he amuse himself by cutting
up these large blocks into little pieces to simulate that construction which was dictated by the smallness of the slabs; or,
resting content with mere appearance, will he make sinkings
where there are neither beds nor joints? In the first case his
construction will be bad and expensive; in the second he will*

utter a lie in stone. In either case his construction will not have style, because it will not be in accordance with the nature of the materials employed, and the manner of employing them in Paris. . . . When you change the material or the method of employing it, you should change the form. When you change the scheme you should change the arrangements of the plan. A moulding has no style in itself; its style consists in its being adapted to the function it fulfills or the place it occupies.

We must endeavour to proceed like the Greeks; they invented nothing, but they transformed everything. Let not our admiration of them limit itself to copying their work as a mere scribe copies a manuscript without reading it; let us read the book and grasp its spirit before transcribing the letter.

Every artist, musician, architect, sculptor and painter may, through a profound knowledge of the resources of his art, and by the right use of reason, imbue his works with style. Even the artist who possesses only sound practical knowledge and is devoid of genuis is capable of comprehending style and of investing his works with this quality which will alone insure their recognition by posterity.

Since the nature of man is one, there is an identity between all the products of his intellect, when the latter allows itself to be guided by truth,—an identity such that certain forms of art always reproduce themselves under the artist's hand; and that the reason of their thus reappearing is that they are true; for it is the characteristic of truth to reach similar consequences by very different paths. . . .

Certainly it is clear that no genuine art can flourish within the range of an architect who confuses the style of the past with contemporary work; who believes that "a good copy" is the best that can be done.

Louis Sullivan said: "Walk for a few blocks through the streets of our city where 'good copies' abound, and you will find a different civilization on every corner and subcivilizations aplenty in between—and yet nobody laughs! What has become of the sense of humor, the keen appreciation of the ridiculous for which we Americans are noted? Everybody would immoderatley laugh if your coat and trousers were not of proper cut and fit. Yet here is an architectural cut and fit far more grotesque than the astronomers of Laputa, with their scholarly ingenuity in doing things upside down. But we do not laugh at the architectural monstrosities, we nod our heads and avow once more that a 'good copy' is the best that can be done!"

Louis Sullivan began the battle in commercial building, but it remained the lot of Frank Lloyd Wright to carry into the field of domestic architecture, as well as into the commercial field, the battle begun by Sullivan. It also became his lot to raise the art of architecture to its true dignity, by demonstrating its organic foundation. As early as 1893 his cry was: "Bring out the nature of the materials, let their nature intimately into your scheme. Strip the wood of varnish and let it alone—stain it. Develop the natural texture of the plastering and stain it. Reveal the nature of the wood, brick or stone in your design, they are all by nature friendly and beautiful. A house that has character stands a good chance of growing more valuable as it grows older, while a house in the prevailing mode, whatever that mode may be, is soon out of fashion, stale and unprofitable. Buildings, like people, must first be sincere, must be true and then withal as gracious and lovable as may be."

An example of the truth of this statement can be seen in one of Dad's first houses, the Robie house at 58th and Woodlawn Avenue in Chicago. Mr. Robie was the inventor of an early engine-driven runabout. The house now belongs to the Chicago Theological Seminary.

Several years ago, the new owners invited Dad to come to dinner and to see for himself how beautiful it still is. Dad asked me to accompany him. He sat at the head of the dinner table surrounded by lovely girls, and beamed. The old brown-stained furniture and woodwork was clean and polished. The soft autumn shade on the sand-finished wall panels had been maintained. The special light fixtures and* leaded glass windows were clear and bright. Even the linen and rugs were in keeping. The owners loved the place and preserved everything as it was originally built. Both warm and sincere was their expressed appreciation.

After we left, Dad said to me: "You see, John, that's an example of a house that has character, it grows more valuable as it grows older. It is good to see care and affection given a work so much a part of me, and into which so much of my early energy flowed."

From the beginning of his practice the question uppermost in Dad's mind was not "What style?" but "What is style?" In 1908 he wrote: "As Americans really demand of the architects a truly noble architecture, we shall never again have the uniformity of type which has characterized the so-called great 'styles.' Conditions have changed! Our ideal is Democracy, the highest possible expression of the individual as a unit not in-

*[JLLW] "geometric" inserted

148

consistent with an harmonious whole. The average of human intelligence rises steadily, and as the individual unit grows more and more to be trusted we shall have an architecture with richer variety in units than has ever arisen before; but the forms must be born out of our changed conditions, they must be true forms, otherwise the best that tradition has to offer is only an inglorious masquerade, devoid of vital significance or true spiritual value."

We who seek broad and convincing aspects of truth know that the Source from which these men received their inspiration did not simultaneously become their personal property. We can make contact with the same Source and acknowledge in our work the one Architecture of which the so-called styles were and are variants expressive of differences and changes in civilization. For architecture now, as ever, is the need and the power to build!

We can look to the great teacher, Viollet-le-Duc; to the great master, Louis H. Sullivan; to the great designer, Frank Lloyd Wright, who embraced the ideals of the teacher and with the inspiration of the master* and his own uncanny ingenuity* blazed the trail through the wilderness to the greater enlightenment of today. Their great works should inspire us with a profound desire, not to imitate, but to emulate them.

*[FLLW] The cat here leaps from the bag—John—in the Teacher-Master-Designer? What does this mean coming from a "son"? N.B. You meant "streamliner"? "Dad"

    [JLLW] What cat?

      What bag?

      Where did he leap?

      "the great teacher

      the great master

      the great designer—what does this mean coming from a son—"

Your rebuke serves me right. I forgot that I was talking about my father who is on earth and gave him the title that belongs to my father who is in heaven—"the great designer." Forgive me father, for I knew not what I did. John

    [JLLW] "We can look to the great teacher, Viollet-le-Duc; to the great master, Louis H. Sullivan; to the great designer, Frank Lloyd Wright, who embraced the ideals of the teacher and with the inspiration of the master" changed to "We can look to the master architect, Frank Lloyd Wright, who embraced the ideals of the great teacher E. Viollet-le-Duc, and with the inspiration of his master Louis H. Sullivan"

*[JLLW] "—all in the light of God Almighty—" inserted

149

18. THE HOUSE BEAUTIFUL*

*The following pages contain the complete text, by William C. Gannet,** of *The House Beautiful*, the book designed by Frank Lloyd Wright and printed by him and Winslow. See page 42.

**[JLLW] "Gannet" changed to "Gannett"

 WITH NATURE-WARP OF NAKED WEED BY PRINTER-CRAFT IMPRISONED, WE WEAVE THIS INTERLINEAR WEB. A RYTHMIC CHANGING PLAY OF ORDERED SPACE AND IMAGE SEEKING TRACE OUR FABRIC MAKES, TO CLOTHE WITH CHASTITY AND GRACE OUR AUTHOR'S GENTLE WORD. APPRECIATION OF THE BEAUTY IN HIS WORK WE WEAVE, —IN PART OURSELVES TO PLEASE, YET MAY WE BETTER FARE, AND, WEAVING SO, WITH YOU OUR PLEASURE SHARE.

F. L. W.

A reproduction* of the ornamental design which appears at the beginning, in between chapters, and on the last three pages. The character of this design indicates Frank Lloyd Wright's evolution from the efflorescent detail of his master's into a simpler character of geometric forms entirely his own. His master's inspiration came from the characteristics of cultivated roses. Frank Lloyd Wright's, from wild flowers.

*[FLLW] Why upside down?

[JLLW] The printer fell on his head—anyway, it's beautiful. John

153

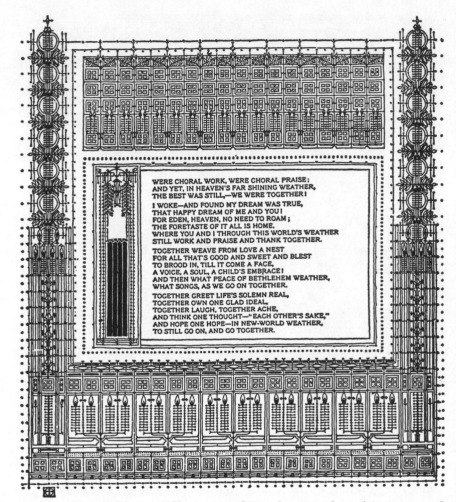

WERE CHORAL WORK, WERE CHORAL PRAISE;
AND YET, IN HEAVEN'S FAR SHINING WEATHER,
THE BEST WAS STILL,—WE WERE TOGETHER!

I WOKE—AND FOUND MY DREAM WAS TRUE,
THAT HAPPY DREAM OF ME AND YOU!
FOR EDEN, HEAVEN, NO NEED TO ROAM;
THE FORETASTE OF IT ALL IS HOME,
WHERE YOU AND I THROUGH THIS WORLD'S WEATHER
STILL WORK AND PRAISE AND THANK TOGETHER.

TOGETHER WEAVE FROM LOVE A NEST
FOR ALL THAT'S GOOD AND SWEET AND BLEST
TO BROOD IN, TILL IT COME A FACE,
A VOICE, A SOUL, A CHILD'S EMBRACE!
AND THEN WHAT PEACE OF BETHLEHEM WEATHER,
WHAT SONGS, AS WE GO ON TOGETHER.

TOGETHER GREET LIFE'S SOLEMN REAL,
TOGETHER OWN ONE GLAD IDEAL,
TOGETHER LAUGH, TOGETHER ACHE,
AND THINK ONE THOUGHT—"EACH OTHER'S SAKE,"
AND HOPE ONE HOPE—IN NEW-WORLD WEATHER,
TO STILL GO ON, AND GO TOGETHER.

Reproduction of last page of text showing the subjective weed frame design in which text is set.

CHAPTER ONE

THE BUILDING OF THE HOUSE*

*[FLLW] Like this act also—

There is a Bible verse that reads, "A building of God, a house not made with hands." Paul meant the spiritual body in which, he says, the soul will live hereafter, but how well the words describe the home,—a home right here on earth!

"EXCEPT THE LORD BUILD THE HOUSE"—

In a sense worth noting, the very house itself, the mere shell of the home, is that—"A building of God, not made with hands." Watch two birds foraging to build their nest. They pre-empt a crook in a bough or a hole in the wall, some tiny niche or other in the big world, and, singing to each other that this is their tree-bough, their hole, they bring a twig from here, a wisp of hay from there, a tuft of soft moss, the tangle of string which the school-boy dropped, the hair that the old horse rubbed off on the pasture bars, and weave and mould their findings into a cosy bowl to hold their little ones. Man and woman are but larger birds, borrowing more of the world-material to make a bigger bowl a little cosier. From a fellow-mortal they buy a lot or a farm instead of a tree-bough; they fence it in and call it theirs, as if they owned the acres through to China,—and put a mortgage on it, notwithstanding, be-cause it is too large to pay for. Then they build four walls with a lid, to box in a little of the blowing wind; screw on this box a door-plate and insurance sign; divide it inside into cham-bered cells; line these cells with paper and carpets instead of moss and horse-hair; and proceed to fill their pretty box of cells with decorations and conveniences. This is their "home." "See what my hands have built!" says the man, but if we look with eyes that do see, what we see is this:—that all he calls his handiwork is nothing but the bird's work; first, a foraging on nature for material, then a re-arranging, re-combining of the plunder.

For consider the house, how it grows! The first thing we do is to dig a hole in the planet,—a socket to hold the house down firm. That is taking liberties with nature to begin with, as we only make the hole, she, room for the hole,—the more momentous matter. Then the cellar-walls—do we make them? We quarry the stone, drag it out, chip it square, lay it in the mortar-beds; but the stone was laid in the quarry for us atom by atom, crystal by crystal, ages before the first man trod the earth. A bit of pavement from Pompeii, a fragment from the pyramids, is prized because man's touch was on it two thousand or thrice two thousand years ago; but each pebble in the chinks of the cellar-wall beneath us holds thousands of thousands of years locked up in it, since first the ancient oceans sifted it and inner earth-fires baked it and thickening continents began to squeeze it into rock.

Then over these foundations we lay the sills and raise the frame. But who made the timber in the joist, who made the clapboards and the shingles on the roof? Men hewed and sawed and split,—the great mills with their iron claws and iron teeth are wonders of human skill; but what hands took sunshine and the rain and a pine-cone a hundred years ago in a wild forest, and with winter storms and spring freshenings and long summer shinings built up the countless cells and fibres

156

into the great green tree, that waited on the hillside till the axe-man came?

And thus we might consider each and everything about our house, the iron in the nail, the wool in the carpet, the glass in the window, the paint on the door, the hair in the easy chair, and trace all back by no long road to builders who built not by hand. We are proud of our nineteenth century mansion; but if we use the very latest improvements and most artificial, — make its outer walls of machine-pressed stone; for inner walls buy fibrous slabs instead of laths and mortar; iron-rib it through and through in place of floor-beams; fireproof its floors with iron netting and plaster; warm it by steam from boilers two miles away down town; light it with electricity; tune it by re-verberating telephones with music played in a distant capital; dine in it, as to-day the city-dwellers may, on fresh fish from the Gulf of the St. Lawrence, fresh beef from Montana, fresh pears from California—still what are we doing but coaxing a little more of world-material from Mother Nature than the forefathers had learnt the art of coaxing from her when they were furnishing their plain log huts? Foraging on Nature like the birds, and re-arranging the plunder, —that is all there is of it.

"I heard a voice out of heaven," says another Bible verse, — "A great voice out of heaven, 'Behold, the tabernacle of God is with men, and He will dwell with them, and they shall be His people.'" Call the great power "God," or by what name we will, that power dwells with us in so literal a fashion that every stone and rafter, every table, spoon and paper scrap, bears stamp and signature to eyes that read aright: "The house in which we live is a building of God, a house not made with hands."

CHAPTER TWO

HOUSE FURNISHING

In this immanence of miracle, this domestication of the Infinite, we have not gone beyond the bare house yet. But how much more than house is home! Cellar and walls and roof, chairs and tables and spoons, —these are the mere shell of the home. These, to be sure, are what the young couple talk much about when waiting for the wedding, and this is what the architects and carpenters and house-furnishing stores are for. And under city slates and country shingles alike, one sometimes finds unfortunates to whom this mere outside, these solid things about the rooms, seem to be mainly what they think of when they think of the rooms; unfortunates to whom the show of their furniture is of more importance than its use; men more interested in the turkey on the table than in the people who sit around the turkey; women who think more of the new carpet than the blessing of the old sunshine; men and women, both, who bear witness that they love their neighbors better than themselves by keeping best things for the neighbor's eyes and worst things for their own, and who almost gauge their social standings by the fine clothes they can put on for street or church, or by the "dead perfection" of their front parlor. Perhaps the good wife, looking around a slovenly, unhome-like living-room, feels a flush of self-respect at the thought of that cold front parlor, where the chairs sit as straight as the pictures ought to, and the tapestries and crockeries are each in the due place. When calling at a rich man's home and waiting for madame to appear, sometimes a silent wonder rises, "Do the people correspond to all this gilt and varnish and upholstery?" And in a humbler house, when shown into one of those polar parlors, a kind of homesickness comes over one for some back parlor, some kitchen, a bed-room, any place where the people really live. The heart cries, "Take me where the people stay; I didn't come to see the chairs." A second thought is apt to follow,—how much more pleasant, tasteful, home-like every other room in the house would probably become, if the expense hidden in this one room were but distributed, there in a prettier paper, there in a quieter carpet, there in a noble picture, and all about in a dozen little graces and conveniences,—if these were added there, where all the time they would be enjoyed by the own-ers and the users. On the other hand, one is sometimes shown into a room, on entering which he feels like bowing to its emptiness in gratitude, because it offers, even bare of the peo-ple who evidently do live in it, a festival so cosy to the eyes. Everywhere are uses in forms of beauty. Uses in forms of beauty,—that is the secret of a festival for eyes. In such cases it is quite in order to sing our little psalm praising the good looks of the room and the things in it that make it pleasant. That is what they are for,—to please; in part, to please us, the chance-comers; but not us first, and the home-folk last—the home-folk first, and us outsiders last. Petition to see a friend's own room before feeling that you really know that friend. It is a better test than a bureau-drawer! Not the room after a quick run upstairs for two minutes first, but the room just as it is. For a room as it is usually kept is index of one's taste, of one's culture, and of a good deal of one's character.

CHAPTER THREE

THE IDEAL OF BEAUTY

I am not objecting one whit to grace in the household furnishings, nor to expense laid out to get the grace. On the contrary, there is nothing beyond bare necessities on which expense may be so well laid out. As the elementary thing that shows one's house is not merely a hand-made house, I would name "taste"; the taste that shows itself in pictures, in flowers, in music, in the choice of colors for the walls and the floors, in the amenities of the mantel-piece and table, in the grouping of the furniture, in the droop of the curtains at the windows, in the way in which the dishes glorify the table, in which the dresses sit on the Mother and the girls. And it is the morning dress and the Monday table that tells the story. Where can you buy good taste? That cannot be manufactured. Like Solomon's "Wisdom," it cannot be gotten for gold, nor silver be paid for the price thereof; but in house-furnishing it is more precious than fine rubies. It is the one thing that no store in New York or Chicago sells, nor can rich relatives leave you any of it in their wills. And yet it comes largely by bequest. Nearly all one can tell about its origin is that it gathers slowly in the family blood, and refines month by month, as children watch the parents' ways and absorb into themselves the grace that is about the rooms.

But what a difference it makes to those children by and by! What a difference it makes in the feeling of the home, if things graceful to the eye and ear are added to the things convenient for the flesh and bones! Our eyes and ears are parts of us; if less important than the heart and mind, still are parts of us, and a home should be home for all our parts. Eyes and ears are eager to be fed with harmonies in color and form and sound; these are their natural food as much as bread and meat are food for other parts. And in proportion as the eyes and ears are fed, we are not sure, but apt, to see a fineness spreading over life. Where eyes and ears are starved, we are not sure, but apt, to find a roughness spreading. A song at even-time before the little ones say good-night; the habit of together saying a good-morning grace to God, perhaps a silent grace, among the other greetings of a happy breakfast-table; a picture in that bare niche of the wall; a vase of flowers on the mantelpiece; well matched colors under foot; a nestling collar, not that stiff band, around the neck; brushed boots, if boots it must be, when the family are all together; the tea-table tastefully, however simply, set, instead of dishes in a huddle, — these are all little things; you would hardly notice them as single things; you would not call them "religion," they are not "morals," they scarcely even class under the head of "manners." Men and women can be good parents and valuable citizens without them. And yet, and yet one cannot forget that, as the years run on, these trifles of the home will make no little of the difference between coarse grain and fine grain in us and in our children, when they grow up.

Besides, this taste for grace is nothing hard to gratify in these days. It is much harder to get the good taste than the means by which to gratify it. Not splendor, but harmony, is grace; not many things, but picturesque things. The ideals of beauty are found in simple, restful things far oftener than in ornate things. Of two given forms for that same article—a chair, a table, a dress—the form that is least ornate is commonly the more useful, and this more useful form will commonly by artist eyes be found the handsomer. A man in his working clothes is usually more picturesque than that same man in his Sunday clothes; the living-room more picturesque than the parlor. "Avoid the superfluous," is a recipe that of itself would clear our rooms of much unhandsome handsomeness. Scratch out the "verys" from your talk, from your writing, from your house-furnishing.

A certain sentence, only eight words long, did me great good as a young man. I met it in Grimm's life of Michael Angelo: "The ideal of beauty is simplicity and repose." The ideal of beauty is simplicity and repose: It applies to everything, —to wall-papers and curtains and carpets and table-cloths, to dress, to manners, to talk, to sermons, to style in writing, to faces, to character. The ideal of beauty is simplicity and repose, —not flash, not sensation, not show, not exaggeration, not bustle. And becaue simple, beautiful things are not necessarily costly, it needs no mint of money to have really choice pictures on one's wall, now that photography has been invented, and the sun shines to copy Raphael's Madonna and Millet's Peasants and William Hunt's Boys and Maidens for us, or the sculpture of an Alpine Valley and a cathedral front. A very little outlay, the dinners cheapened for a month, will make the bare dining-room so beautiful that plain dinners ever afterwards taste better in it; it really is economy and saves a course.

CHAPTER FOUR

FLOWER FURNITURE

And without any money at all, what grace the fields and gardens offer us, if only we have eyes to see it, hearts to love it, hands to carry it home! I knew a woman, among friends counted poor, whose room was a place to go around and praise and be thankful and delighted for, so much did she have of this faculty of transferring nature to the inside of a house. Mosses and ferns and dried autumn-leaves were her chief materials; but the eyes and the hands and the taste were added in, and rich men could not buy her result. To be a growing flower anywhere is to be beautiful. "Consider the lilies," said the young Hebrew Prophet; and when we do consider them, we want some of them nearer than the field. The Arabs put into Mohamet's, their prophet's, lips the saying: "If a man find himself with bread in both hands, he should exchange one loaf for some flowers of the Narcissus, since the loaf feeds the body indeed, but the flowers feed the soul." Flowers have no speech nor language, but they are living creatures, and, when transplanted from their own home-haunts to ours, they claim the captive's due of tenderness, and they will reward love, like a child, with answering loveliness. In their religious rhyming to the woods and fields outside, the seasons faithfully remembered in captivity, their wondrous resurrections, their mystic chemistry that in our corner bedrooms carries on creation, constructing green leaf and glowing petal and strange incense out of earth and water and the window sunlight, the little exiles of the flower-pot bear mute witness that the house wherein they live is "a building of God, a house not made with hands."

CHAPTER FIVE

BOOK FURNITURE AND OUR GUESTS

We must say a word about two other things, seldom thought of as house-furnishings. One of them is our books. Think what a "book" means. It means meeting a dime-novel hero, if we like that kind of hero. But it also means meeting the poets, the thinkers, the great men, the genuine heroes, if we like that kind. It means admission to the new marvels of science, if one choose admission. It means an introduction to the noblest company that all the generations have generated if we claim the introduction. Remembering this, how can one help wishing to furnish his house with some such furniture? A poet for a table-piece! A philosopher upon the shelf! Tyndall and Darwin, in their works, for members of the household! Browning or Emerson for a fireside friend! Irving or Dickens or George Eliot to make us laugh and cry and grow tender to queer folk and forlorn! Or some of the good newspapers, — not those that, on the plea of giving "news," parade details of the divorces and murders gleaned from Maine to Florida, details of the brute game of the prize-fighter and the shames of low city life, — not this red, rank meat to hang around one's mind, as if it were a butcher's shop; but newspapers that tell how the great world is moving on in politics and business and thought and knowledge and humanity. To subscribe for one of these last is truest house-furnishing. A family's rank in thought and taste can be well gauged by the books and papers that lie upon the shelf or table in the living-room. There are three or four books which a man owes to his family as much as he owes them dinner or clothes, — a good newspaper (that is, one new book daily), a good dictionary, a good atlas, and, if he can possibly afford it, a good cyclopaedia. A boy asked his Mother a difficult question, and got the answer, "I don't know." "Well," said he, "I think Mothers ought to know. They ought to be well educated, or else have an encyclopaedia." That boy was right. And if we own no more than these four books just named, they are four presences to day and night remind us that their house and ours is a house not wholly "made with hands."

Another thing which passes manufacture is our guests. They are surely as important a part of the household furniture as the chairs we buy for them to sit on. A house that merely holds its inmates, and to the rest of the town is a barred place, good, like a prison, to keep out of, can hardly be a "home" to those who live in it. It must be pleasant to a woman to know the children like to look up at her windows as they run to school, hoping for her smile; it must be a pleasure to a man to know the neighbors look forward to an evening around his fireside or a chat and laugh over his tea-table. The truest hospitality is shown not in the effort to entertain, but in the depth of welcome. What a guest lovest to come, and come again, for is not the meal, but those who sit at the meal. If we remembered this, more homes would be habitually thrown open to win the benedictions upon hospitality. It is our ceremony, not our poverty, it is self-consciousness oftener than inability to be agreeable, that makes us willing to live cloistered. Seldom is it that the pleasantest homes to visit are the richest. The real compliment is not to apologize for the simple fare. That means trust, and trust is better than fried oysters. One of my dearest haunts used to be a home where we had bread and butter for the fare, and the guest helped to toast the bread and wipe the dishes; but the welcome and the children and the wit and the songs, and the quiet talk after the children went to bed, made it a rare privilege to be admitted there. If the dinner be a loaf of bread and a pitcher of water, invite your friend rather than incur that opposite reputation, that it is "a kind of burglary to ring your doorbell before dinner." Count guests who are always glad to come and always make you glad they come, as best pieces in your household furnishing; and those who are glad to come, without the power of making us so glad, —count some of these as reasons why the house was built.

CHAPTER SIX

THE DEAR TOGETHERNESS

And still one thing remains to furnish The House Beautiful, —the most important thing of all, without which guests and books and flowers and pictures and harmonies of color only emphasize the fact that the house is not a home. I mean the warm light in the rooms that comes from kind eyes, from quick unconscious smiles, from gentleness in tones, from little unpremeditated caresses of manner, from habits of fore-thoughtfulness for one another,—all that happy illumination which, on the inside of a house, corresponds to morning sunlight outside falling on quiet dewy fields. It is an atmosphere really generated of many self-controls, of much forbearance, of training in self-sacrifice; but by the time it reaches instinctive expression these stern generators of it are hidden in the radiance resulting. It is like a constant love-song without words, whose meaning is, "We are glad that we are alive together." It is a low pervading music, felt, not heard, which begins each day with the good-morning, and only ends in the dream-drowse beyond good-night. It is cheer; it is peace; it is trust; it is delight; it is all these for, and all these in, each other. It knows no moods—this warm love-light,—but is an even cheer, an even trust. The little festivals of love are kept, but, after all, the best days are the every-days, because they are the every-days of love. The variant dispositions in the members of the home, the elements of personality to be "allowed for," add stimulus and exhilaration to this atmosphere. Shared memories make part of it, shared hopes and fears, shared sorrows; shared self-denials make a very dear part of it. Thus is it at its happy best; but even when the home-love is not at its best, when moods at times prevail, and cold looks make a distance in the eyes, and some one grows recluse and selfish to the rest, even then the average and wont of love may keep the home not wholly undeserving of its coronation name, "a building of God, a house not made with hands." Certainly love is the force by which, and home the place in which, God chiefly fashions souls to their fine issues. Is our mere body fearfully and wonderfully made? A greater marvel is the human mind and heart and conscience. To make these, homes spring up the wide world over. In them strength fits itself to weakness, experience fits itself to ignorance, protection fits itself to need. They are life-schools in which the powers of an individual are successively awakened and trained as, year by year, he passes on through the differing relations of child, youth, parent, elder, in the circle. From the child's relations to the others come obedience, reverence, trust,—the roots of upward growth. Youth's new relations bring self-control and self-reliance, justice, and the dawns of duty owed one's world. Later, when little ones in turn demand our care, mother-providence and father-providence emerge in us, and energies of self-forgetting, and the full response of human nature to the great appeal to be good for love's sake. Lastly, old age with its second leisure and dependence brings moderation, patience, peace, and a sense of wide horizons opening. And, all the process through, love is the shaping force, and home-relations are the well-springs of the love. If this may be called the story of soul-making for us all, of none is it so mystically, beautifully true a story as of the blessed "twos." Mystically true of them, because the love of twos begins in miracle, and the miracle never wholly dies away even when the days of golden wedding near. A mystery like that of birth and that of death is the mystery of two young spirits all unconsciously through distant ways approaching, each fated at some turn, some instant, to find and recognize the other. Follows, then, the second and continuing mystery of the two becoming very one. And beautifully true of them—as all beholders know: "All men love a lover." Poetry and song, and novel and drama, and gossip, older than them all, attest the fascination. But to the two themselves how passing beautiful the story is! It is not merely that all nature glows and old familiar things take on new lights and meanings; nor merely that in the new light the dearest old ties dim by some divine eclipse,

> "As o'er the hills and far away
>   Beyond their utmost purple rim,
> Beyond the night, beyond the day
>   The happy princess follows him."

Not merely this: a higher beauty comes in the changes so swiftly wrought by love within each soul,—the enlargement of powers, the enhancement of attractiveness, the virtues greatened, the meanness abated, and that unselfing of each one for the other's sake, which really makes each one a stronger, nobler self. The sunrise of the new life breaks. The two are mated with the solemn questions: "Wilt thou love her, honor her, cherish and comfort her, in health and in sickness, in joy and in sorrow, so long as ye both shall live?" "Wilt thou take him for richer, for poorer, for better, for worse, and try to live with him the divinest life thou knowest?" Then begin the daily, hourly answers to these questions,—living answers so different from the worded "I will" of the moment.

And now the home-nest, and the delights of it, the discoveries of it, the revelations in it of still unmated parts which yet must mate and will, the glad endeavors of it, all begin. Now poems, only making dear a printed page a little while before, sing themselves out as glad experience:

> "Two birds within one nest;
>   Two hearts within one breast;

> Two souls within one fair
> Firm league of love and prayer,
> Together bound for aye, together blest;
> An ear that waits to catch
> A hand upon the latch;
> A step that hastens its sweet rest to win;
> A world of care without;
> A world of strife shut out;
> A world of love shut in!"

Slowly the new home grows holy as the deepening wedding thus goes on; holy, for the making of two souls—two yet one —is going on in it. Each soul is overcoming its own faults for love's sake, and helping by love to overcome the other's faults. Business, sorrows, joys, temptations, failures, victories, ideals, are all shared in it. By and by the awes of motherhood and fatherhood are shared, and the new co-education that children bring their parents is entered on together. The supreme beauty is attained when both realize that the inmost secret of true marriage is—to love the ideals better than each other. For this alone guarantees the perfect purity, and therefore this alone can guarantee the lastingness of love. Literally, literally so!

> "I could not love thee, dear, so much,
> Loved I not honor more."

Emerson's words are the motto for all marriage-chambers: "They only can give the key and leading to better society who delight in each other only because both delight in the eternal laws; who forgive nothing to each other; who by their joy and homage to these are made incapable of conceit." And so the divine end of beauty is fulfilled—the purification of souls, the ennoblement of personality.

By far the best love-story that I know among the books is a true one, "The story of William and Lucy Smith"; a sad, triumphant love-story that leads the reader far along the heights of life and death. These two had no children at their side; they had no wealth to buy them graceful things; their very roof they could not call their own; and they only lived eleven years together. But they lived these years a lofty life in all the full sweet meanings of together. "Togetherness" is the quaint word in which Lucy tried to sum and hint the happiness.

So when I think of The House Beautiful, "the building of God, not made with hands," I think of them. He said to her, looking up into her face not long before his death: "I think you and I should have made a happy world, if we were the only two in it." She said of him, closing the little memoir that she wrote: "Of him every memory is sweet and elevating; and I record here that a life-long anguish, such as defies words, is yet not too high a price to pay for the privilege of having loved him and belonged to him."

> I dreamed of Paradise,—and still,
> Though sun lay soft on vale and hill,
> And trees were green and rivers bright,
> The one dear thing that made delight
> By sun or stars or eden weather,
> Was just that we two were together.
>
> I dreamed of heaven,—and God so near!
> The angels trod the shining sphere.

And all were beautiful; the days
Were choral work, were choral praise;
And yet, in heaven's far shining weather,
The best was still,—we were together!

I woke—and found my dream was true,
That happy dream of me and you!
For eden, heaven, no need to roam;
The foretaste of it all is home,
Where you and I through this world's weather
Still work and praise and thank together.

Together weave from love a nest
For all that's good and sweet and blest
To brood in, till it come a face,
A voice, a soul, a child's embrace!
And then what peace of Bethlehem weather,
What songs, as we go on together.

Together greet life's solemn real,
Together own one glad ideal,
Together laugh, together ache,
And think one thought—"Each other's sake,"
And hope one hope—in new-world weather,
To still go on, and go together.

19. ISAIAH'S O.K., DAD

I HAVE SAID Dad is not a good teacher. In one sense he's the best, for he says and does things that provoke the spirit of investigation. The Isaiah tirade in his Autobiography brought this individual to my attention.

It seemed that each time some disaster overtook Dad, even when one of his prize cows was struck by lightning, he thought that guy Isaiah was about again. I wanted to know who this boo could be for I was getting some bad breaks myself. I looked him up and found he ministered in the kingdom of Judah, attacking the corrupt national life. Religious scholars say that nowhere else in the literature of the world have so many colossally great ideas been brought together within the limits of a single work as in that one known as Isaiah. He was a great prophet, statesman, teacher, a man of wisdom, eloquence, of literary genius with inspired insight and vision. And with all this he enjoyed a happy, compatible married life and had two sons. He believed that the power of quality rises above quantity.

The thing that struck me was the similarity of his ideas to those of Dad's. Isaiah was a hellion against foreign alliances, especially in the time of danger. And Dad says: "The less we ally ourselves with alien forces—the more nature will smile upon our efforts to build a future greatness . . ."

Perhaps Dad developed a psychological quirk when he was forced to memorize the fortieth chapter of Isaiah while yet a child. Yet, with his natural inclination for the beautiful, I wonder why he did not select a line for his theme, such as "Comfort ye, my people . . ." or "The word of the Lord thy God will endure forever."

Dad quotes Scripture: "The flower fadeth, the grass withereth . . ." He believes that Isaiah deemed the flower less desirable because it seemed to have been condemned to die. I cannot see that Isaiah intimated that the short duration of the flower diminished its value, took away the sweetness of its perfume, the brilliancy of its colors or the exquisite delicacy of its petals. It seems to me that he was comforting his people. The frail things they loved could disappear, but that organic truth which created them in the first place is with them always.

It may be that his love for the flowers prejudiced him, for I cannot remember when he did not surround himself with the lovely things. The last time we visited him, Taliesin was a bower of pine branches and anemone, wholesome and fragrant as the woods themselves. The perfume of burning oak in the seventeen stone fireplaces—the aroma of red apples and shagbark hickory nuts drifted to the threshold when we entered. Here was a beauty we could feel and smell as well as see —the beauty of simplicity. Dad was busy as usual, yet not too busy when "the Priestess" expressed the wish to have some anemone, to spend most of the day with us, poking about the surrounding country, sweet for acres with the scent of it.

But Dad doesn't like that word "woe." He says that word "woe" struck on his young heart like a blow. He believes that

Isaiah's awful Lord smote the poor multitude with a mighty continuous smite, never taking away the gory, dreadful hand outstretched to smite more, never satisfied with the smiting he had already done. Verily, he believes that this holy warrior was a prophet making God in his own image. Turning his own lusts into virtues because they were on the side of pain instead of pleasure. Then he says, "What a curse to put upon the mind of a child."

To that spasm I say: "Whoa, Dad!" You can't fool me. I know you too well to believe that anything could be put upon your mind that you did not want there.

Isaiah was not condemning the people to an awful death by a wicked lord. His condemnation was directed to the corruption which pervaded Babylon. He, like you, used strong words to denounce the old and perverted form. Along with "Storm Center Architect" that I used to call you, I could well think of you as a modern Isaiah, for Isaiah never uttered words with greater vigor. To make my point clear, I quote at random from your writings:

"Here at hand was the typical American dwelling of 1893 standing about on the Chicago Prairies. That dwelling became somehow typical . . . but it did not belong there. I longed for a chance to build a house, and soon got the chance because I was not the only one then sick of hypocrisy and hungry for reality. . . .

"What was the matter with the house? Well, first for a beginning, it lied about everything. It had no sense of unity at all nor any such sense of space as should belong to a free people. It was stuck up in any fashion. It was stuck on wherever it happened to be. To take any one of those so-called 'homes' away would have improved the landscape and cleared the atmosphere.

"This *typical* had no sense of proportion where the human being was concerned. It began somewhere in the wet and ended up as high as it could get in the blue. All materials looked alike to it or to anybody in it. Essentially this 'home' was a bedevilled box with a fussy lid; a box that had to be cut full of holes to let in the light and air, with an especially ugly hole to go in and come out of. The holes were all trimmed, the doors trimmed, the roofs trimmed. . . . It is not too much to say that as an architect my lot was cast with an enebriate lot of criminals, sinners hardened by habit. . . ."

"Radio City, Last Tower of Babylon is the crime of all crimes and there is no excuse for it whatever." You denounced its builders as men who abused their commercial privileges by robbing the citizen of his right to a simple life.

"Look at the thing!" you declared, speaking of the Empire State Building, "not as it says it is or as it would like to be, but as it is—an unethical monstrosity, a robber going tall to rob neighbors." Your large audiences of prominent people sit, for the most part, in shocked silence as you select your targets and proceed to demolish them.

Now what would you say if one of those shocked persons would write: "Frank Lloyd Wright's awful idea of architecture smote down the multitude of houses, the dwelings of people, the buildings of men, with a mighty continuous smite, never taking away the gory, dreadful hand outstretched to smite more; never satisfied with the smiting he had already done. And he will not be satisfied to stay his hand till every edifice he calls 'lying hypocrite' is razed to the ground."

I myself have heard your burning words and have seen the prophetic fire in your eyes as you denounce. In such moments you not only resemble Isaiah, but also Elijah when he drew down fire from the sky to confound the priests of Baal.

You have said: "A single glimpse of reality may change the world for any of us." I am convinced that you have had this single glimpse. But Isaiah had it two thousand years before you. Your words today, are precisely similar to those he used yesterday. Had they been heeded then, you would have more receptive hearts to respond to your efforts now.

Had you been living in his day you would have called him a "free thinker" for he, like you, was a great soul on fire in a great cause. He did not believe in dogma, his neighbors called him "lax" and "unreligious." He was again like you in that he often preached but did not attend the preachings of others, and he had a great admiration for the nursery. His cry was, "Get the heart of a child within you." He tried to raise the people to a level from which they could appreciate nobler dwellings than those they had.

He believed in decentralization too. He denounced the crowding together of dwelling places just as you do, only he said it this way:

"Woe unto them that join house to house, that lay field to field, till there be no place that they may be placed alone in the midst of the earth."

That's why I say, "Isaiah's O.K., Dad."*

*[FLLW] O.K.—John

20. HEAD MAN*

DAD PRODDED his Lincoln Continental in the upward climb, up on over the heights between the peaks; up on toward the stars; on toward the Great Silence. "Come now, be a good sport," he coaxed, "we haven't much farther to go."

"I refuse to run on your reputation! Give me gas!" it sputtered. Dad shaded his eyes with one hand and peered ahead like an Indian chief. All of a sudden he found himself where he wanted to be. The Lincoln suffered one last convulsion and quit!

Wearily Dad climbed out, fumbled in the back seat for a thick, red book which he tucked under his arm

"I can't make a grand entrance like this. St. Peter will think I'm licked." He drew himself up to his full height—swung the end of his long, black cape across his chest—took his Malacca stick in hand, tossed his head into its usual pose and turned in the direction of the gate. Several feet from it he stopped, swung his cane forward till it reached the bell and gave it a poke!

"Who's there?" came a voice from behind the gate.

"Frank Lloyd Wright—"

"What do you want?"

"I want gas." His skylark eye caught the proportion of the gate. "Ah ha," he hummed, "there will be some changes made." The "tired" left him, he took a few jig steps, swung about and whistled a triumphant little tune. The voice behind the gate rushed to St. Peter breathlessly:

"Mr. Wright—Mr. Frank Lloyd Wright, waits without!"

"Without what?"

"Without gas!"

"Greet him and tow him in! No, don't do that—wait—I will greet him myself." St. Peter swung open the golden gate. "So it's you again, Frank, what brings you here?" Dad was puzzled, when had he been here before? He bowed gallantly to St. Peter.

"It's I, all right, I give you myself."

"Why?"

"I can't get what I want when I want it!"

"What do you want?"

"Gas! I have three Lincoln Continentals, and fifteen Bantams and I can't run any one of them. But that isn't all, Peter, I'm tired, too. Now let's get down to business. Is this a permanent place? Is one compelled to stay once he enters?"

"By no means. Some of our guests go back and forth, one moment they're here, the next—they're in hell."

"Hmm," Dad raised his eyebrows, "not altogether unlike the place I just came from."

"It is similar, but that shouldn't surprise you. The Good Book says 'on earth as it is in Heaven.'"

"So it does, it sounds interesting—I think I shall come in—" his gaze now roamed to the towers of the buildings. "Yes, you need me here—these gates, those towers—monstrosities!"

"Tut, tut, tut," singsonged St. Peter, heading him off with

upheld hand, "not so fast, young man, not so fast. You have no 'reservation,' as you call it on earth."

"I want you to know that I get accommodations merely by presenting *myself*."

"You do on earth, Frank. On earth it is in this, your defiant spontaneity, that your special charm lies. That's one reason I advise your returning. The ones who get accommodations here, merely by presenting themselves, are those who have given up their earth life in the terrible struggle down there. They are admitted immediately and are made comfortable and happy. They are all free to return to earth whenever they choose. But they are having such a good time not one of them wishes to do so. Look, Frank, why don't you go home, at least until this busy season is over?"

"Peter, that's the reason I should come in, the young folks all like me, I will join them in the merrymaking. I will build spacious rooms and make them livable. From what I see I don't wonder that your guests go to hell for a change. We've got to raze the whole thing to the ground and start over."

"Tut, tut, tut," St. Peter stopped him. "You can't crash the gate this way, what can you show for yourself?"

"Utterly ridiculous," snapped Dad. "You, yourself, greeted me as friend and called me by name."

"We greet every one as friend, and you announced your name." St. Peter shook his head. "I see you're accustomed to having your own way—but you know, Frank, you can't run this show. You're not Head Man here!"

"I only want to be of service," Dad replied mildly.

"Well, then, let's waste no more time—show me your credentials."

Sweeping the air with a grand flourish, Dad drew from under his cape the thick red book. "Who's Who in America" was printed across the cover.

St. Peter invited him to be seated—*outside the gate*! With an air of patience Dad obeyed. St. Peter opened the book, turned its pages to "W's" and ran his finger down the list. "Hmm, hmm. 'W' 'WR' 'WRI' 'WRIGHT'—Wright! Yes, here it is. 'Frank Ayers Wright, Architect—Liberty, Sullivan Co., New York."

"No, no!" Dad jumped to his feet. "I am Frank *Lloyd* Wright!"

"Sorry—let's see—'Frank James Wright, Geologist'—tut, tut, tut." His raised hand stayed the impatience of the now irrate Dad. "'Frank Lee—Frank Lloyd . . .'" With a sigh of relief, Dad sank back in his chair.

"'FRANK LLOYD WRIGHT, Architect, Born Richland Center, Wisconsin, June 8, 1869;* Son of William Russell Cary and Anna Lloyd (Jones) Wright; . . . Began practice at Chicago, Ill. 1893; Architect of Imperial Hotel, Tokyo, Japan and numerous other buildings of note; work characterized in America as "The New School of the Middle West," and in Europe as: The American Expression in Architecture . . .

Hon. Mem. Academie Royale Des Beaux Arts D'anvers 1927;
Extraordinary Hon. Mem. Akademie Der Kunst (Royal Academy) Germany;
Hon. Mem. Instituto Central De Architectos, Brazil;

*[Editor] In 1946, JLLW accepted the date of his father's birth as 1869 instead of 1867 as subsequently discovered by Thomas S. Hines.

Hon. Mem. Royal Institute of British Architects, Great
  Britain;
Awarded Royal Gold Medal for Architecture by King
  George VI, 1941.
Honorary Member, Uruguay National Academy.
Honorary Member, Cuba National Academy.
Honorary Member, Mexico National Academy.
Honorary Member, Holland National Academy.
Honorary Member, Switzerland National Academy.
Honorary Member, Japan National Academy.
Honorary Member, Russia National Academy . . .'"

St. Peter paused for breath, scanned the unending list. "Why,
Frank, there are thirteen books of which you are the author
. . . fifteen books written about your architectural achievements . . . hundreds of articles praising your work in leading
magazines and newspapers all over the world . . . I needn't
read more—I admit, you have a neat pile of assets."

"By way of information," Dad smiled, "that isn't all. I play
like Beethoven, I dance like Astaire, I love like Casanova . . ."*

"Hallelujah!" ejaculated the voice. "That man has had too
much heaven already—he needs a little hell. Why don't you
get Mephistopheles on the phone, St. Peter?"

"That's a good idea." St. Peter dialed the gate phone:
H-E-L-L. "Hello Meph, you red-hot rogue. Can you accommo-
date Frank Lloyd Wright?"

"Christ, no! I couldn't have that guy down here—he would
disrupt the whole damned place in no time. The whole of hell
is parceled out in twenty foot lots with no restrictions. We have
a tendency to 'huddle.' We tip everything edgewise. We have

*[JLLW] "Casanova" marked for deletion

182

the cutest little bungalows and Georgian gems with suffocating attics and dark dank basements. The furnishings are Louis XIV, XV, XVI—Chippendale, Hepplewhite and Sheraton. Our roofs are ridged, tipped, swanked, gabled, becorniced and bracketed. We have corner-boards, panel-boards, corner-blocks, plinth-blocks, rosettes, fantails, jigger-work in general. Our shops are jumbled, our main street dark and narrow. Hundreds of congested, squalid little lanes radiate from it. Every building down here is in strict accord with popular abuses.

"Our business houses are Roman, Greek, General-Grant-Gothic. All structures are pilastered and entablatured—candle snuffer domes, spires, inverted rutabaga radish and onion. The chimneys are lean and tall, their sooty fingers threaten heaven itself. Hell, no! Don't send him here."

St. Peter turned away sadly. "No, Frank, you can't get in there either. You are too good for hell, but not good enough for heaven."*

"Be a good sport, Peter," coaxed Dad. "Let me in, just for a little while, I promise not to cause trouble."

St. Peter hesitated.

"I don't like to chase you home Frank, let's look at you in our record. Maybe we can find some justification for your coming in temporarily." St. Peter opened a cabinet and tugged at an immense book. Drawing it out he laid it on the desk, turned to the page "Frank Lloyd Wright." Dad's curiosity got the better of him; he peeped over St. Peter's shoulder—across the top of his own page, "*Isaiah*" stood out in bold type.

"Why does Isaiah's name appear on my record?" demanded Dad, "can't I get rid of that bogy even up here?"

St. Peter burst into a hearty laugh.

*[JLLW] "You are too good for hell but not good enough for heaven." changed to "You are too bad for hell and too good for heaven."

"A man can't get away from himself, Frank, and it's always himself that causes him the greatest disturbance. You see, you were *Isaiah*. You left here in 765 B.C., to prophesy against the great Assyrian monarchs, and boy how you went after them—they've never been the same since! The Head Man was proud of you and gave you a good long rest when you returned.

"In 1694 A.D. you wanted to be a philosopher, to write books and plays and have more glamour than your Isaian life afforded. So you chose the wife of a French notary to bear you. You were broadly known as *Voltaire*, and mingled in the brilliant court circles of Louis XIV. But you retained the Isaian fervor and made written attacks against the powers-to-be that earned you imprisonment for eleven months. Your first writing was publicly performed and received with favor. This brought you recognition and substantial financial profit. But you could not overcome your use of free invectives nor the habit of insulting the powers higher up and so to prison again you went. From there you were sent to England where you were deeply affected by the toleration of free thought—so much freer from the traditional stamp of Louis XIV whom you secretly hated.

"Later, you bought a country house in the republic of Geneva and built a large and beautiful private theater on the grounds where your plays could be performed. Always seeking a way to freedom you wrote freely attacking religious fanaticism, political institutions and intolerance, and always in the defense of sovereignty of reason.

"In 1778 you returned. You were here only ninety-one years when the urge to be an architect overcame you. The Head Man has in every age sent at least one soul to earth to witness the fact that human ingenuity is superior to human cruelty. Walt Whitman witnessed this through poetry—Louis Pasteur through medicine—Edison through electricity . . . and so on through the long list. The urge in you was so great that He decided to try, this time, through architecture.

"He did not release you until He found one Anna Lloyd Wright, who desired that out of the depths of her being would burst the flames of genius in architecture. The Head Man heard her prayers and directed you to unite with her. You left us in 1869. But it didn't take you long to start an upheaval.

"It is clear that your qualifications have earned a place for you in heaven, but you can't come in, not now, not now— you have unfinished work. Why don't you go home?"

"I'll go to hell first, I'll not go back to earth. At least, not at this particular time. Furthermore, what unfinished work holds me out?"

St. Peter patiently resumed: "Humanity is tiring of walls built by mistaken ideas. You were chosen as a leader to break through the walls of tradition, conventionality and formalities by presenting the ideal of organic architecture on earth."

"I have been doing that for more than fifty years."

"Yes, you have, Frank, but that is not the point. You do a good job building your buildings in keeping with your ideal. But you have been weak in your support of others in their desire for this same attainment. Although there is nothing to show that you ever depressed or quenched any rising genius, neither can there be shown that you ever stood behind one and helped him up.*

"You speak of a young man who is the best example of what Taliesin can do for a young apprentice and what a young ap-

*[FLLW] Guilty!—who ever did that thing? Don't be silly— John, the thing never happened because it would be utterly <u>unnatural</u>, therefore <u>impossible</u>!

prentice can do for Taliesin. How long is a young man young, Frank? After ten years his work with you inspired in him so great a love for farming that you can no longer get architecture out of him or into him. To take an apprentice to make him an architect, and then brag about his becoming a farmer is not in accordance with the 'plan.'"

"Plan, hell!" interrupted Dad. "The education of an architect should commence when he is 2 days old, 3 days is too much, and Peter, I've said it on earth, and I'll say it in heaven: *No one should be an architect who can be anything else.*"*

"Tut, tut, Frank, and a couple more tuts; your work, among other things, is to encourage students to become architects—not exclusively by way of you—forever attached to you, but in their own right.

"No one knows better than you that all great architects have in some way been released from dependence upon their masters at an early age.* Truth in architecture, as in any other line, is not solely the property of any one master or school."

St. Peter scanned the ledger again. This time he wiped the wet sadness from his eyes. "Oh, Frank, woe, woe, there's a black mark on your record—you fired your boy John! You fired him because he outwitted you."*

"Woe is me—I rue the day I begat that brat—from his infancy he has thought of little else in life save new ways in which to torment me. Now he causes the one black mark on my record! I should have known that I could not get rid of that boy by firing him.

"Peter, I've got to come in, I'll tell you all. I did not come here because I couldn't get gas—I did not come because I'm tired. I came because that nemesis is writing a book about me.

*[FLLW] Check
[JLLW] double check
[Editor] On the original, quotations are next to a bracket embracing this paragraph.

*[FLLW] (Not me)

*[FLLW] Oh yeah!

I do not want to be around when it comes out—if you don't mind, I'll come in. I promise to go home quietly after it blows over."

"No, Frank, you wouldn't be happy here, not even for a little while. The dwellings would harass you. Our guests build their houses of intangible stuff, patterned from the houses they lived in on earth. There is nothing you could do to change them. Then too, you could build but one house here—your own. On earth you can build for others. If you teach them to lay hold of the principle, they will build in harmony with your ideals.

"You have already made earth life less barren, but you must carry your work further. Send your students out on their own to build and expand. Tell them that they can tap the Universal Brain as you have. Be glad if you so inspire them with your genius that they emerge with ideas that transcend—*even yours*! Do not block your own path by insisting upon passing everything Organic through yourself first, as though you were the only architectural organ on earth. Do not attempt to be the Source that is your source. And, Frank, when it comes to poetry . . . you'll be safest with Walt Whitman . . ."*

"Where am I?" Dad questioned. His eyes now open rested on his own objects of art. His glance strayed to me. He sighed with relief. "I'm so glad you're here, John, what brought you?"

"They called me, Dad, you had been asleep too long. I'm glad you awakened. Come on, get up, the war is over. The young people have returned, they want you to build Broadacre City—they are not satisfied with things as they have been."

*[FLLW] Silly my boy—If I had to tell 'em that—it would be no use. Little Johnny speaking to poor old Dad.

[JLLW] Not silly—not to "poor old Dad," but little Johnie (sic) speaking from heaven to his father who is on earth. John

[Editor] Both comments refer to the whole paragraph, as indicated by brackets penciled on the original by father and son.

Dad's face brightened, his voice took on a new dimension. "I'm glad you wakened me, John"; he held my hand tightly. "I want to tell you something that has been on my mind for a long time. I am sorry I fired you for collecting your pay."

"That's all right, Dad. When I think of those days, had I been you, I would have fired me sooner."

"No, John, you were a good boy; always looking after my interests; always overfed, but underpaid."

"It was my fault, Dad."

"No, John, it was my fault, but I'll make good. We shall build Broadacre City. You shall receive five hundred dollars each week and all expenses paid."

"Wait a minute—not so fast! Let us not start that all over . . ."

"Honest, John." One eye winked shut. With his hand cupped like a telescope over the other, he peered at me. "I shall put the money in escrow. All you need do is to go to the bank and get it . . ." Dad's voice grew stronger and stronger —louder and louder: "Five hundred a week . . . five hundred a week . . . get it . . . get it . . .!"

A clap of thunder sat me straight up in bed. Dad began to disappear, fading backward as it were. One eye still peered at me, but the voice now droned,* "Forget it . . . forget it." I cupped my hand over one eye, and gave him an answering wink.*

*[JLLW] "droned" changed to "grew softer and softer"

*[FLLW] Little Johnnie's Humor? <u>Back to the money again!</u> But still humorous—money always is.

21. BY THEIR FRUITS*

> . . . Many a saint in the making seems to be marred by faults and conflicts from which the smug, careful, reputable sensualist is exempt . . .
>
> HENRY VAN DYKE

*[FLLW] The best chapter in the book, John—and well placed—<u>Dad</u>!

WHEN YOU TURN a spotlight on an object, you can at best see only the outer shell. Newspaper headlines, gossip, scandal, succeeded only in showing up a distorted shell of my father, portraying him to the world as the matrimonial gargoyle and champion bad-dad of the U.S.A.

There is little wonder that some persons, viewing him in that light, have come to the conclusion that he led an immoral life. His life has been one of color, of sorrow and achievement, of disappointment and joy, but not one immoral. In so far as orthodox codes are concerned, he was sometimes immorigerous; rude, uncivil, disobedient, yes, but never immoral.

My great* grandfather was a Roman Catholic bishop who was excommunicated, even from social intercourse with the faithful, for marrying a redheaded girl. He fled with her from England to America.

*[JLLW] "great" changed to "greatest"

My grandfather was a Protestant preacher who excommunicated himself from several denominations, even from social intercourse with his wife and children, and fled* to—no one knows where. My father was one of his children.

*[JLLW] "fled" changed to "vanished"

It is folly to exact from, or demand of a man that which he has not the capacity to fulfill.

189

Morals are dependent upon a variety of changing things, so there is no permanent moral standard. During the time of Moses the code was "an eye for an eye and a tooth for a tooth." The Poet of Peace asked us to give our coats when we're sued for our cloaks. If we do not follow His code, why moralize at all?

Bernard Shaw once said that you can do anything you want to do if you talk strongly enough the other way, and say anything you want to say if you act strongly enough the other way. In connection with this Dad says, "Intelligent people who love the truth of life and seek reality only seem to live to be frustrated." Then he adds, "I don't mean the intelligentsia or the highbrow. The highbrow, as my old master said, was merely a man educated far beyond his capacity."

Our laws get better all the time because in the past many of them have been outrages to human decency. Maybe tomorrow the laws of today will be considered such outrages. Dad says, "Naturally laws will be abused where they interfere with life and try to assume responsibility which they have no business to assume in any decent society. Only where culture is based upon the building of character by freedom of choice will we ever have the culture of true Democracy."

Dad did not believe that virtue always depends upon following the strict conventions of the world without even questioning whether they are right or wrong. He did not regard a precept as right by reason of the world's proclaiming it so, without reflecting as to whether it was right in itself. He could see in life, as in architecture, that the laws and conventions are based upon rules making no allowance whatsoever for the individual circumstances of the case. And to conform to con-

190

ventions that he felt in his soul were wrong, to him was not a virtue but only cowardice.

About eighteen years ago Dad said to me, "I want to be 'regular,' but I would rather be truly alive irregular, than regularly dead. I am irregular simply because I got out of step with the procession and—not being permitted to come back into the ranks—blazed a trail for myself in the direction I imagined the right way to the goal all were marching toward, when circumstances forced me to quit. I might have laid me down then and given up what was life to me, sincerely, and to others, but I didn't. I made my own way forward. That in itself is, boiled down to first principles, my connection with the immoral class. The faith that is in me may be unable to go with laws, but it is never lawless."

Yesterday, Dad made good headlines for bad purposes. Today he makes modest news items for noble purposes. Yet the remembrance in the minds of many is the headlines.

"Names have been my undoing, not acts," says Dad, "except as the acts too are *named*, instead of being allowed to show their nature for themselves. . . . I got off the train on the wide western prairie once upon a time at a pretty village named Mount Royal. I asked a citizen where the mountain was. He shrugged his shoulders and gave me a contemptuous look as he said, 'Aw—that's just the *name*.' But *names* seem to make history for the gentle reader; indeed, I suspect now that all history was more or less similarly made. Let no one take names lightly in an age, at a time when all are taken in vain or not at all."

When, in this era of names and naming, my thought turns back through the years and I review the picture of our home life, I can find no instance in Dad's fatherhood in which he failed one of us. His mental and moral character was of the highest quality. During the eighteen years of the happiest kind of family life he was loyal and devoted; never scolded, never criticized, never nagged or punished. He did not smoke or drink. He neither swore nor gambled. He loved life, loved his work, loved people, loved flowers, loved trees, loved the beautiful. He was cheerful, worked hard and played hard. And then one day, he fell in love—in love with some one other than our mother.

All the scandalmongers and moralizing mumblers in the world cannot destroy the beauty through which two persons find love and have the courage to face what may lie before them, renounce all else if necessary to give it holy expression. If marriage is the only custom through which two persons can give holy expression to their love—then the condemnation could only be justly laid at the door of those who block their path and make it impossible for them to express it through marriage. My father's open declaration was not necessary had he not wanted more than anything else to give his love holy expression. But circumstances would not allow him to do this, so he followed his heart, and paid the price.

"I am neither poseur, liar nor charlatan," he says, "but it is my misfortune however that I believe in Santa Claus and in this I have often found myself in a hellafajam. There have been times when it appeared that I had outraged the outrageous more outrageously than the outrage was itself outrageous."

Many faults have been found in connection with various stages of the life of this man of magnificent ego and sweet sentimentality. But could it be other than a greater weakness that would choose a man's weakness to characterize his whole personality? Do we measure the value of the garden by its weeds? Do we measure a tree loaded with good fruit by a broken limb?

Alexander Woollcott expressed the sentiment of many when in 1930 he wrote in an article which appeared in the *New Yorker*, "Indeed, if the editor of this Journal, were so to ration me that I were suffered to apply the word *genius* to only one living American, I would have to save it up for Frank Lloyd Wright."

Not long ago I received a letter from a young law student who is a lieutenant on a patrol craft overseas. He wrote: ". . . Last night I read some from *The Collected Legal Papers of Oliver Wendell Holmes*. There, was truly a great lawyer. He was to American law what Frank Lloyd Wright is to architecture, Monet and Henri were to painting, Beethoven to music, Carrel to medicine. It is so obvious when reading, seeing, or hearing the works of great men — irrespective of their fields — that the one spiritual unity is what makes them great." From my many contacts with the younger generation, I know that in the substantial thought of the youth of today, Frank Lloyd Wright stands for high-minded achievement.

The other night* I met Dudley Crafts Watson at the Cliff Dwellers. "I saw your Father a week ago," he beamed. "With the poise and bearing of a god, he walked into my studio in the Art Institute." Mr. Watson's face flushed with excitement, his voice rose to a higher pitch. "Yes, in walked this magnificent man, wearing the most exquisite overcoat I have ever seen. His tie, an overtone of bronze, completed the most

*[JLLW] "The other night" changed to "In 1945"

exciting ensemble I have ever laid eyes on. 'In times like this, Frank, how do you manage to get these splendid materials?' I asked, fascinated by their quality. His handsome head with that shock of white hair was held high. Glowing with youth, bristling with health, he said to me, 'Wait till you see the blueprints of the Guggenheim Museum. It's going to stand on Fifth Avenue, almost directly across from the Metropolitan Museum. It's going to make the Metropolitan look like a Protestant barn'—and out he breezed."

Today at seventy-six, Frank Lloyd Wright is a living, breathing, active and powerful chieftain, still going forth conquering and to conquer. He is happily at work in the present, for the future—still far ahead of his time. Like Beethoven's Eighth Symphony, the scenes of his life shift and change and a skylark emerges singing rapturously in a kind of special melodic consciousness, and lesser themes go chasing helter-skelter to give the Chief a rest before the final verse.

No checkered account will obliterate a rebel, a jolt to civilization, whose romantic theme—purposive planning, and organic unity in inventing and combining forms—is an epoch in the architecture of the world. No checkered account will obliterate the love in the heart of a son for his Father who is on earth; and—by his fruits shall he be known.*

*[JLLW] <u>Again</u> this chapter saves the book—and John—<u>Dad</u>

FROM

GENERATION
TO

GENERATION

FRANK LLOYD WRIGHT*

*[FLLW] What a horrible looking monster! . . . serves me right? <u>Dad</u>

[JLLW] Anyway—He will always be "Mr. Class" to me, holy gee! John

Additions to an
Intended Edition,
1962

"Special Problems That Befall a
Son of a Great Man"

Postscript

Additions to an Intended Edition,
1962

Foreword to Revised Edition

With considerable anxiety I awaited word from my father after sending him "My Father Who Is On Earth," the first book that I had ever sent him that he had not read before. A week passed before the postman handed it back to me. A few tense moments were followed by feverish haste in tearing open the package. Between the covers lay a sheet of his colorful paper on which was written: "Dear John: Herewith ungracious comments marked on the Opus-itself—as I read: Kindly send me another one—will you? Hope you and Frances are happy and get some fun out of it all—Love Dad. Frank Lloyd Wright April 2, 1946."

My relief was complete for Dad used the word "Opus" only when he likened something to a pleasing musical composition. From then on no ungracious comment jolted me greatly!

On the fly leaf on which appear the lines "If the character in this book resemble anyone living or dead . . ." Dad wrote: "And John—they do, in a way quite your own—yes, I appreciate the affection you express for your next-to-the principle character—(for I share it for you) but—of all your 'characters' I think you have done the principle one (yourself) best—and this is as Autobiography out to be—else why the thing at all—? There is some truth in it tho—and Dad hopes you will get some money out of this (on the whole) a well-written washing of family linen—soiled—but not so dirty as one might think?—I think your book will sell.— Whistler once called attention to the fact that he could take care of his enemies but prayed the Lord to deliver him from his friends—and this being nearer than 'friends' is much worse for me? Yes? As the plot thickens, life grows more interesting— however. Yes? Dad."

199

JOHN LLOYD WRIGHT

My father's running comments through the book were a mixture of tranquillity, primeval humor and thought prevalent with shock. At the end of chapter, "Isaiah's O.K. Dad" in friendly agreement Dad wrote, "O.K. John." In the margin of Architectonics: "Good Stuff" and "Thanks son." M. Viollet-le-Duc was "a good act." The chapter "He Fired Me" brought Mars and all the lesser planets flying past me at once. The words of Dr. Schevill, father's best friend, rang in my ears. "Come on with it, your father may not like everything in it, but why should he?" And yet, somehow, I hoped he would. To put it mildly, Dad did not approve of certain portion of this chapter, they were pointless and lacked dignity. With this view I am in full accord and have been sorely tempted to omit the chapter entirely. My decision not to abandon it came as the result of considering what else would have been expected? To Dad, there must be contrast. If all comments followed in an even tone, there would be no contrast, no sequence, no progress, merely a continuation like a building all in one dimension. To Dad, this would be "ignominious." I have added material to this chapter which points out my father's courage under pressure. Perhaps when all is said and done it is necessary to read between the lines for truest light.

The brevity of Dad's praise of the last chapter moved me: "The best chapter in the book and well-placed." At the end of this chapter he wrote: "Again this chapter saves the book, — and John, Dad."

During a long private talk in his Arizona studio, the first time I visited him after he read the book, it was obvious that some things that I thought funny were not so funny to others. It was also obvious that "on the whole" my father was well pleased with the book, had read it many times and liked it as well as he liked anything he did not write himself. And so, the book goes forth again with foreword, technical revisions, additions and addendum.

JOHN LLOYD WRIGHT
Del Mar, California

Three Insertions

Chapter 5, p. 58, to begin chapter:

In my father's autobiography he recounts: "I remember: The third week after I first left my first home in Oak Park the misery that came over me in a little cafe somewhere in Paris. Caring neither to eat or drink, I was listening to the orchestra. It had been a long depressing rainy season, the Seine most of the time over its banks. And it was late at night.

The cellist picked up his bow and began to play Simonetti's Madrigale. Lloyd had played the simple antique melody often. I would sometimes play with him, on the piano.

The familiar strains gave me one of those moments of anguish when I would have given all that I had lived to be able to live again.

The remembered strains drove me out of the cafe into the dim streets of Paris with such longing and sorrow as a man seldom knows. I wandered about not knowing where I was going or how long I went, at daylight finding myself facing a glaring signboard—somewhere on the Boulevard St. Michel. I remember: . . . . . . So, I will remember to forget most of what I intended to write."

This struck a cord in me, for the year Dad left home I etc.

Chapter 12, p. 94, comments:

By comments in the chapter, my father indicates that in his mind incidents leading up to the Inouye episode were responsible for my being "fired,"—not money. He felt it "not fair," "not true," for me not to recite such events in relation to my being fired. Even if it were possible to write the whole story, it would take a whole book to do so, and even then not be worth reading, as the story would be too repetitive of difficulties inherent in youthful marital adjustments since the beginning of the world. At the time both my father and myself were in the throws of marital problems. Before leaving for Japan I had surprised him by taking on a wife (entirely on my own) and he had surprised me by taking on a mistress — later a wife — (Mirriam — sic — of the "Frankie and Johnnie" chapter, — entirely on his own). By his request, I had left my wife behind when we went to Japan. He had taken Mirriam (sic) with him. Shortly thereafter, while he was back in America, I requested my wife to join me in Tokio (sic). She came. It was not long after her arrival that Mr. Hayashi (the Manager of the Imperial Hotel) called me in for a fatherly heart-to-heart talk. Among other things he said my wife was not the girl for me and would I send her back to America. I said, "No, my wife is young and I want to work out a life with her. If my wife goes, I go too." Mr. Hayashi wrote to my father (I learned later) saying that if I would not send my wife back alone that he thought it best that we both should go back. This happened just prior to the money episode that concluded my employment and found us both back in America. A divorce shortly thereafter testified to my inability to "work out a life with her."

At the time of writing my book, I thought I had covered the situation in the chapter "Head Man" by saying, "That's all right, Dad. When I think of those days, had I been you, I would have fired me sooner." It did not do so. Anyway, this story is the missing link that brought on my father's comments in the chapter "He Fired Me."

Chapter 12, p. 98, to accompany the first note:

I remember particularly one time when the fate of this hotel was at stake. At issue was not merely whether an architectural design would be turned down or accepted; more important by far was the fate of countless numbers of people whose life, limb and property were to be saved by this building from future destruction by earthquake. The Imperial Hotel's Board of Directors had been frightened by adverse criticism from an American architect plying his trade in Japan. There was nothing in the engineering books to support my father's design. There is never anything in the books until some one puts it there.

A conference was called to clear up the fear. It took place between Baron Okura, who represented the Imperial Royal Household's controlling interest, and my father, late one night in the Baron's private study in his impressive Tokio residence. An Interpretor [sic] stood by.

I knew my father's professional caution would make it impossible for him to take chances. I knew he was right, for each time a tremor occurred I had measured its effect upon the experimental loaded piles which we had set up on the property. But could he convince the Baron that his conception would work in the complexities of the entire structure? The air was tense, my nerves tingled. My father was fighting for his life. "We are building on ground which the seismograph shows is never still for a moment,—we must prepare to meet it by other means than rigid force," he began. "If there is more awful threat to human happiness than earthquake, I do not know what it can be." There was no movement nor sign of expression on the face of the Baron. "Human beings are maimed, trampled and crushed," my father pleaded, "when without warning a quake comes along it grabs hold of the foundation and snaps it like a whip. We cannot fight the quake, we must outwit it." He signaled to me and I spread the drawings on the floor. He explained in detail the plan he had formulated to float the building on the mud cushion, free of the rock strata below, much as a ship floats on water.

Several hours passed. Difficulty after difficulty thinned away. The fate of the Imperial Hotel was determined when the Baron rose to his feet and said to my father, "Go ahead young man."

After the great quake of 1923, when the news was heralded around the world that the Imperial Hotel stood undamaged, my father calmly remarked, "It is the triumph of good sense."

Chapter 12, p. 98:

In the Architectural Record, April 1923, the great architect, Louis H. Sullivan wrote, ". . . a high act of courage—an utterance of man's free spirit, a personal message to every soul that falters, and to every heart that hopes . . . the Imperial Hotel stands unique as the high water mark thus far attained by any modern architect. Superbly beautiful it stands—a noble prophecy."

[Editor] JLLW repeats here the second note he penciled in on page 98.

Addendum

Without losing the gain of earlier experiences I have had the benefit through the past fourteen years of a bigger more mature view of my father. This resume through varying scenes up to and through the final verse is simply an expression of my appreciation of him whom the world knows as Frank Lloyd Wright.

Every age produces a few men who are termed "Source Minds," who tune in to the Source from whom creative ideas flow and thus enlarge the resources to be embodied in future work. Frank Lloyd Wright was one of the few in our age. From the start his poetic thought characterized his work with a sincerity and simplicity of expression that moved the hearts and pleased the eyes of those weary of architectural artificiality. This distinctive feature places his work in the domain of art where it will continue to exercise a profound and direct influence upon the development of the generations to come.

On page 33 of this book I wrote, "I have often wondered if his inspiration for 'Broadacre City' did not come from Walt Whitman's 'Song of The Broad Axe.'" On the margin of this page father wrote, "No, the Song came from the same place,—that's all." It has been of value to me to know that my father was aware of drawing everything of beauty directly from the Infinite in spite of his disconcerting delight in placing himself first.

My father had the heart of a child within him and to the end, except in his architectural work, was easily influenced by those with whom he had close contact. On page 35 I mentioned his five draftsman who made contributions to the pioneering of Modern American Architecture for which my father received the full glory headaches and recognition. In answer to this he wrote in the margin, "Many suffered in silence that I might glitter—I know! I know!" One of the silent sufferers was my beautiful mother, Catherine Lloyd Wright, his first wife and mother of six of his children. Mother encouraged, inspired and helped father through the first nineteen years of his practice during the time he established himself as a great architect. Perhaps it is because my father passed away two weeks after the death of my mother that as I write I am compelled to salute my mother also, for her inspiration is to be found in the foundation of the architecture my father left to the world.

Frank Lloyd Wright was an American idea that pressed irresistibly toward fulfillment. His skill was acclaimed by far seeing minds who had risen above ordinary conceptions of architecture before the turn of the century. Intuitively or otherwise they grasped lofty and lasting truths in the unity of his daring handling and recognized that here was a revolutionary who had already given us a new kind of space. From that moment on his work was a standard by which great architecture is measured today.

Had my father's truly brilliant period ended here, he would not have been world-renowned, but his place through time in the history of architecture would have been just as secure. As my thoughts drift back to this period, I recall my father surrounded by admiring clients and a prank-loving family who adored him. Later I doubt if he could have gone on as he did were he not the Orb, encircled by satellites who constantly supported his ego, for he found in them the human sympathy that every great egoist needs.

During the time I worked for my father his presence was a mixture of euphoria and crises. He was a series of surprises; was expert in getting himself in tight positions, delighted in being confronted with difficulties. In his broad alternation of moods ran the whole gamut from pathos to rapture, and withal he had a witching sort of magnetism. Somewhere between this multiplicity lay the magic of the man. One day he remarked, "Things seem to be going along too smoothly,—things are too quiet." His anxiety was always unfounded for the quiet never lasted. The memory of those delicate situations has faded but not so the central experience of exposure to his mind. Like a river, he was incessant, unexhausted. If it so happened that I wearied, his sharp eye caught it in my work. His swift pencil hovered over my clean drawing like a hummingbird. Then in a spring of quick action it descended and began its fatal strokes. The result, surprising each time, culminated in striking revelance of detail peculiar to him. "Be faithful in the little things, get joy into your work," he reminded when he softened away harsh lines, "Humanity will best love creative work characterized by joy."

At times my father was full of quiet philosophy. To him, a work of art was a great deed of happiness, nothing more or less than one's sense of action when one is touched by truth. He made it clear that all the truly great periods were those whose architecture had in it an inherent relation to the physical and soul life of the people.

By piecing together his scattered profundities it became evident to me that America's national feeling has been struggling for a century against absortion through yielding to the foreign influence; that architecture is the utterance of the sincere living spirit of the people; that true form is a quality that results from an organic process, not a prescription. He said he was not a teacher, but I learned from him that the architect who merely reproduces facts of life without adding to our compensation of it,—without supporting it by all the weight of his spiritual experience,—love, tenderness, joy, is not an architect at all. He is merely a cerebral activity. An Architect is a man with a spiritual inheritance that he uses to direct the thought process.

My father's keen eye caught and assimilated every beautiful thing into himself. He imparted to it a touch of his own quality which in its origin it did not possess and it would come forth in fresh interpretation,—a chain of vigorous strongly knit forms of remarkable beauty, each growing out of the other. There was never a striving for effect but the effect was strong and true, for it came naturally out of cause. By observing him I could see that one's own unpremeditated quality cannot be carried out by others, that each must develop his own quality and get it into his work; that wherever a man's creations show principle at work it is not imitation regardless of its form, for the working of principle behind effects within the same spatial and temporal environment naturally produces similar effects. One helpful observation was that the ideals to which my father dedicated his life, were trampled upon before his time, during his time and this will continue until destruction is no longer tolerated in the minds of men. Meanwhile, the determination to destroy, only serves to insure a more definite way to preserve, for truth has a persistent quality.

It was a bleak day when I left my father's office, but it was good for my growth for it compelled me to search for the spiritual equivalent of the indescribable aesthetic pleasure his personal communication meant to me. Whatever happened later, working for my father for five years gave me a solid foundation, an understanding of the organic ideal and deepened my reverence for it.

I have never known a man with greater versatility than that of my father. With equal ease he could violently antagonize, seal confidence, express the sarcasm of Voltaire, the humor of Twain, and from me evoke the belly laughs of W. C. Fields. When I smarted under his criticism in tender solemnity he said, "When I criticize your work I do it out of affection. A man who does not love the things he criticizes can't criticize honestly." Perhaps if his criticism were more widely understood as affection, there would have been less antagonism and fewer hurts.

It is understandable that my father's methods for education received little attention. Not long before he died he hurled a one sentence lecture to the students of one of our Universities, "Throw away your text-books and get out of here and look at nature." So saying he held his elegant head high and removed his respectability from the tainted atmosphere. While it is fatal to put technique above inspiration and it is true that the Creative Spirit passes beauty out to every one by way of nature, no one knew better than my father that architecture involves something in which text-books have a place. I doubt if any man could perform like this and not be called "an ornery cuss," "A baffling erratic." Some of his infuriating quips came from the pain of his own scars, but more sprang from the same impulsive overwhelming imagination that caused profundity to appear in his work. Like Mark Twain, he knew you could "edit the trivia out, but you cannot edit greatness in," and father remembered everything whether it happened or not and forgot everything he did not wish to remember.

ADDITIONS TO AN INTENDED EDITION, 1962

One of my father's determinations was to make architecture and at least one architect known throughout the world during his lifetime. This, he did. "Honest Arrogance" made good news copy and beside, he said humility was unbecoming to him. But his childlike delight in public approval set me to wondering if he had the humility in him that did not allow him to realize his importance in the world of architecture. I recall his open joy in the Royal Gold Medal awarded to him for Architecture by King George VI, and feel safe in saying he treasured it above all tardy ones that came pouring in at long last. To look at it put him in a bouyant mood. On several occasions he removed it from its velvet case, bounced it in the palm of my hand that I might feel its weight. "That's a real solid gold medal," he applauded with a twinkle.

Within Frank Lloyd Wright's strong and rugged forms is a tender love of life. "No house is a machine for living except as the heart of man is a suction pump," he warned. Since he was the father, not only of modern architecture, but also of the new freedom of space, he felt a deep responsibility for the modern trend that revels in the abuses of that freedom. He did not conceal his contempt for the conscious stress on trick effects that mingled his geometric forms with heterogeneous bedlam. He called it "The International Quilt," and "Architecture A La Mode." Several years ago at the conclusion of a press interview, my father called after the departing correspondent, "To hell with modern architecture."

While my father made no dramatic proclamation of his regard for other living architects he had respect and affection for sincere and honest men in the profession. He was particularly shy when it came to complimenting his children. But then, for some reason inherent in nature, lions display monumental indifference toward their cubs. Nevertheless, one of my treasured mementos is the article he wrote, which appears on pages: 114, 115, 116, and another is a letter in which he wrote, "High regard for you and your work along similar lines makes you a friend for whom we solicit continued support and interest in any way you feel free to give it . . ." My appreciation for the basic quality of this friendship will be preserved as long as I live.

JOHN LLOYD WRIGHT

On April 6th [1959], I was notified of my father's illness. I called the hospital in Phoenix and asked to speak with Frank Lloyd Wright. "Room 447 is in surgery," came the reply. My heart sank. Had my honestly arrogant father been reduced to a number? I insisted on reaching one of the doctors who informed me that the operation had just been successfully completed. As late as the evening of April 8th, I was assured, "He is holding his own." The rasp of telephone bell at four A.M. said otherwise. "He just sighed and died," the nurse in attendance reported later. I had always thought of my father as eternally young, living on and on. A great void was suddenly present, wistful regret, inner combat. How could I best pay tribute to him now? How could I express the pulsing gratitude I felt for the inspiration he had been to me. As I sat stunned in the hush of darkness his voice came clearly through the silence of eternity. "John, my boy,—never mind the merchandise (which he termed the lifeless body), go on in your work,—let nothing interfere with it."

When daylight broke, a bewildering chase of stray memories accompanied me as I drove to one of my buildings under construction. As I walked into the structure I felt my father's hand on my shoulder. There was a surge of encouragement from him that seemed to permeate the entire atmosphere. The tradesmen who had all heard the news over early morning radio expressed a kindness of spirit beyond anything I had experienced before. As I left the site, the kaleidoscopic tragedy and pathos of his life crowded in upon me. The chief actor of an historical drama was gone. Gone was the man who in my youth exerted on my mind a compelling and romantic spell; who recognized the beauty of the works of the past, yet lived in a world of today and cared for its simplest weeds; who hoped that all wild heroisms would some day be directed to peace and upbuilding of beauty; who started a work in the middle-west of America that found its way to the far corners of the earth. Gone was the man whose philosophy, like that of St. Augustine's, was love truth and do what you like, for what you like increasingly alters as you grow to love truth. Was a shadow of a joyous symbol all that remained? As often happens when one descends, there comes a light that leads to freedom,—

210

a return to steady course. I felt tears smart my eyes but I no longer felt forlorn.

Shortly after the death of my father a Memorial Panel appeared in the ground floor galleries of The Museum of Modern Art, New York. Mr. Arthur Drexler, Director of Architecture and Design was kind enough to send me the text which I reproduce here:

FRANK LLOYD WRIGHT 1869–1959*

There is no aspect of modern architecture that Frank Lloyd Wright did not anticipate or realize during his astonishing 72-year career. His death, on April 9, 1959, at the age of 89, occurred while he was still actively engaged in those innovations with which he transformed our conception of architecture.

So many of Frank Lloyd Wright's ideas have become part of our environment that we often forget their origin. The open plan and sweeping horizontal lines of his early prairie houses; the exaltation of the natural qualities of materials; the siting of buildings as if they were extensions of the landscape; the unending variety of forms and techniques with which he created architecture more timid men might have thought unbuildable—all these things have influenced the appearance of our buildings and even the way we live in them.

Throughout his life Wright sought to devise an architecture that would express the ideals of American democracy. He chose to heighten the quality of life by providing settings in which the individual could grow and change. His stress on the importance of the individual carried into the twentieth century something of the exuberant romanticism of the nineteenth.

Frank Lloyd Wright was unquestionably the greatest of American architects. But his stature is not only national; he has affected architecture throughout the world. He was not only one of the great figures of the twentieth century; he was one of the truly original architects of all time. (A.D.)

* [Editor] FLLW was born in 1867.

JOHN LLOYD WRIGHT

Frank Lloyd Wright was a true giant of the age. He was born with the love of architecture in him. From his early childhood his eyes were trained to see, his brain to think, his hands to do. He not only had vision, he had the ability to execute his visions. With his concept of depth interpenetrating depth, he brought to life the philosophy of Laotze, "The reality of a house is the space within to be lived in." This brought about a freedom in design not known before but which today is employed by every good architect in his designs throughout the world. This in itself made him a liberator of architecture and is a lasting tribute to his genius. But whether it be in the field of art, commerce or humanity in general, we have all benefited from the genius of this rebel and the benefits are beyond comprehension. But as my father has wisely put it, "We have a talent for letting great men disappear except as memorials, and our monuments are made by those who never did anything but betray the thing the great man loved most."

I, for one, will not let my father disappear if my goal is "the true" rather than "the new" if I am compelled by my own inner vision, not discipleship. My father often repeated, "A native culture is doomed by discipleship, a disciple is an everpresent detriment, a graft that takes sap from a parent stem. Even the most faithful disciple could be only a handy expedient for business."

The passing of Frank Lloyd Wright leaves a deep hurt within me, yet it is not the end of goodness or greatness. Life demands that we go forward with wisdom and understanding. To remain dependent upon the personality that the person himself transcended through struggle, rather than upon the ideal, is to stagnate. In every field of endeavor it is necessary to receive a new revelation of truth from time to time. In fact, it is inevitable. There is one sign of greatness not difficult to detect,—a work however simple, beautifully done.

The man who thus indoctrinated me was rhythm, bittersweet harmony, joy, storm, tragedy. My appreciation to him for my entry into the world in an atmosphere where talent was taken for granted is great. My appreciation of Frank Lloyd Wright's gargantuan legacy to the architecture of the world is still greater. A salute

ADDITIONS TO AN INTENDED EDITION, 1962

to the man of poetic energy, of tempestuous motion, of romantic sentiment. A salute to him who drew beauty from the Infinite to bring into the world that will last forever.

JOHN LLOYD WRIGHT
Del Mar, California

213

"Special Problems That Befall a Son of a Great Man"

PLACED ON A PEDESTAL in Rome, is an equestrian statue by Bernini of the Emperor Constantine who had his father-in-law hanged, his brother-in-law strangled, his nephew's throat cut, his wife smothered in a bath, and his favorite son beheaded.

All through ancient history sons of great men were beheaded, hanged, thrown into dungeons and pitched into the sea. The more tender hearted of the great fathers just quietly smothered them.

In the words of Genghis Khan, "There can not be two suns in the heaven nor two Khans on the earth." If son escaped with his head, his problems were not over. Enemy camps got busy to "give him the works." In those dark days sons lived as fugitives until hunger drove them to desperation. They made a dash for freedom, only to be pursued by angry rivals.

And so,—down through the centuries in the maddest whirl of clash and din, in the tramp-tramp of booted feet, in the wild splash of the sea, the ill-boding whine of the wind, we hear the haunting cry of the special problems of the sons of the great. They are not much changed today. History repeats itself, the methods differ. How delightful, the elusive bitter-sweet quality of it all.

But my conscience won't let me write another line until I define my terms. To me, "great" stands for something quite different from "famous." Great men need no applause to satisfy an inner doubt concerning their power and ability. Men who become "famous" often do so through their insatiable appetite for ego glorification;—a need to be reminded by the crowd that they are above the crowd. Genghis Khan was in a panic at the thought of leaving something for anyone else to conquer. If there is something in the world of architecture yet unconquered, my father is on his feet like a shot with a horde of recruits following. He will leave no opportunity for posthumous bestowal.

214

With this off my chest, I vision myself peering slantwise at a stone-slab on which is carved: "HERE LIES JOHN LLOYD WRIGHT, ACCIDENTALLY SHOT AS A MARK OF AFFECTION BY HIS FATHER." Of course, the special problems depend upon the length of time the son lives. Son John feels that he has made the grade to have lived long enough to celebrate the eighty-eighth birthday of his father.

MY FATHER'S DOMESTIC LIFE has posed many problems for this son. There was a constant struggle between the head and the heart. I first remember him as the head of our household, owned by the family. Second, I remember him owned by a ladylove he desired to marry but could not because my mother would not let him. Third, he was owned by a poetess from Paree, or someplace, whom he inadvertently married when my mother let him. Fourth, he was owned by a beloved object whom he married after adjudication of unique complexities and by whom he has, I thought, remained owned. The fifth shock was when he told me he was owned by a Foundation.

In relation to the problems which are the legacy of this son, there are triumphs, failures and a world of laughs. I seldom think of my father without the picture coming to mind of the vulnerable veteran actor who, every time he heard a clap of thunder, strode majestically to the window and took a bow.

If It's Good, He Did It

My father's devotees, spurred by his own pronouncements, discount all ability other than his own. When we built our studio in Del Mar, California, sight-seers came from far and wide. Soon, rumor was abroad that my father designed it. Some persons came right out and asked, "Did your father design this house Mr. Wright?" If it's good, he did it. Why say more.

Recently, I received a post card picturing in color a Resort Hotel. Printed lines gave credit to my father. A client mailed it to me contributing one line: "John, this should not happen to you." When the publisher discovered the error he sent a package of cards with over-printed correction. My father's name was blocked-out and mine inserted. I can not use the cards for my father's name is slightly visable through the over-print. To some persons this would mean, without doubt, that I had usurped one of his works.

An anecdote which appeared in a Chicago newspaper expressed a phase of this problem. Ashton Stevens wrote: ". . . Lloyd Lewis suggested to Jed Harris that son John could build Harris just as Wrightworthy a house as his Dad could build him. To this brilliant sales talk in behalf of son John, theatrical producer Harris answered, 'People of my faith believe in the father rather than the son.'" I am certain that my father concurs with Mr. Harris, for I heard him say to one of my clients, "Why fool around with the coupon, when you can have the bond."

If I could get the twinkle into my writing that is in my eye, I could tell here that some people have told me that they like my work better than my father's. But since I can't, I don't dare repeat it.

THERE ARE THOSE WHO HAVE EXPRESSED WONDERMENT for my courage in entering architecture. Since I was nineteen years old, there was nothing else that I could do. I did not enter the arena by way of my father. In 1911, I was in California. My father knew not where I was nor what I was doing. In 1913, I sent him photographs of my design for the Golden West Hotel in San Diego and my first house in Escondido. It was not until then that he knew I had entered architecture. His answer was an immediate invitation to join him in his Chicago office, which I did. I worked for him for five years during the time I could best serve him.

FRANKLIN D. ROOSEVELT JR., I am told, decided early in life to exploit the rich legacy of his father's name rather than fight it. I had no such legacy to exploit. When I chose architecture, I felt it my responsibility to add weight to the name for at that time my father was infamous, not famous. I had nothing to look forward to by way of his public relations. The black front page headlines were not about his colossal achievements but rather about his colossal escapades. Harold Bell Wright was the public idol of the days.

THE GREAT WALTZ KING JOHANN STRAUSS reigned supreme when his son entered the field of music. My father did not reign supreme when I entered the field of architecture, unless perhaps as the man who built "freakish houses." Father Strauss threatened, admonished and forbad his son to play the violin. My father threatened, admonished and forbad me nothing. One day Father Strauss stormed out of the house to his mistress never to return. So did Papa. Mother Strauss fired the boy's ambition to play the violin and left no stone unturned to back him up and arrange for his public debut. It was of no concern to my lovable Irish mother what work I chose, so long as I worked. Johann would have nothing to do with his father because it was his mother's wish. My mother did not approve of my working for my father, but I could not grant her this wish. My admiration for my father's work was too deeply rooted in me. The "pull" was too great.

It did not occur to me that later in life my father's genius would be known throughout the world. Nor did it occur to me that, whether the son comes close to the spirit of the father, it matters little. The same problem exists in overcoming public misconceptions. If what son does is good, father had handed it out to him. Resistance to this is extermination. How to cope with this problem was then the situation. Son must either make something real of himself or be blotted-out. There is no middle course.

AFTER I LEFT MY FATHER'S OFFICE, the sudden separation from the warp and woof of his rampant life left me floundering for awhile. Of course, if I were like Alexander the Great, who was even more ambitious and energetic than his father, I too would have wept bitterly to hear of my father's conquests for fear there would be no worlds left for me to conquer. But this son was not interested in conquest. His interest was to earn his living and while so doing to find enough good qualities tucked away in him to justify his existence. He would start by making some contribution in order to feel his own strength, not a competitive one, and yet,—it must be allied with architecture. This urge resulted in something that brightened the hours of millions of children throughout the world. His invention of the construction toy, "LINCOLN LOGS" is known today as America's National Toy.

JOHN LLOYD WRIGHT
There Are Diversity of Gifts but the Same Spirit Works in All

In a biography by John A. Garraty, we are told that Henry Cabot Lodge's son George was hindered by the help of his father and his father's friends. ". . . Lodge and Theodore Roosevelt bombarded magazine editors with his poems, 'nothing so good had been written in English since Shakespeare, friends of the family declared.'" Unlike the experience of George Lodge, to presume that a son of my father has a God-Given gift or even a thought of his own is heresy in some circles. In others he is under the weight of exorbitant expectations. Whatever he does is compared with the achievements of his father rather than upon an appraisal on its own merit. A contribution need not be spectacular to be sound or lasting.

My father does spectacular things in order to bring about spectacular changes. Thomas Edison once said that in every generation there is a handful of what he called "source minds" — men who create ideas that are the model and inspiration of thousands who come after them. To this select group, I would without hesitation nominate my father. I feel that I have a specific work to do, like a part in a play. If I do my own work well, I can respect myself and gain respect from my audience. Not by trying to steal the show from my father, but because I have put everything into my part that could be put there.

THERE HAVE BEEN FLEETING MOMENTS WHEN MY FATHER HAS EXPRESSED REGARD for my work. Yet if praiseworthy publicity is afoot, into my ear come low rumbling sounds, "the more tender hearted of the great fathers just quietly smothered them." A series of strange paroxysms follow which do not readily abate. But since I understand him, his insistent reiteration that I am an ass, and that all that is good stems from him, loses much of its ominous sting. If enemies pursue, the cacophony blossoms into a herald call, "John, I'm coming down there and clean them up." "Ambivalence," best describes the indefinable emotion. My experience in this respect is not unique. In "Knight Errant," a biography of Douglas Fairbanks, Jr., Brian Connell tells us that for most of the second decade of his life young Douglas was subject

218

to his father's "almost pathological opposition to his development as a screen personality; and in his third decade fought an uphill battle to win the confidence and friendship," of his father. Neither his father nor mine originated "ambivalence" even though they were victims of it.

However, unlike Douglas Fairbanks, Jr., I had no desire to fight a battle to win my father's confidence or friendship. I know that I have as much of them as he is capable of giving to anyone. It would be folly to expect from him more than he has to give. At one time, my father's disinterest in my work depressed me. But I soon realized that he was so engrossed in himself that there was little left for me, except as I might be useful to him in attaining his aim. This realization, during his march to fame, has saved me many a private heart-ache.

Poetic License

One day, while showing my father a school building, his eye caught sight of the corner-stone on which my name was carved. "John, my boy," Dad said, pointing his stick at the name, "Why the name—the building itself should identify it's architect." "Dad," I replied, "except for the name, some one might think you were the architect,—and I seem to remember a big block of sandstone laid in the wall of the Hillside Home School on which, 'FRANK LLOYD WRIGHT, ARCHITECT' is carved."

"That should not be there," Dad quickly retorted. "Timothy, the Welsh Master-Mason, did that on his own and placed it when I was not around. When I came upon it, the old man was so proud of it, so filled with sentimental emotion, tears in his eyes,—and it was so beautifully cut, I could not move myself to tell him to take it out." I understand that now he has porcelain red-squares on which are his initials, for the purpose of placement on all of his buildings, past, present and future.

Unpredictable

The part I played in the Midway Gardens Project in Chicago was important to my father. But not nearly so important as the responsibilities that were mine in the Imperial Hotel Project. And yet, in connection with the Midway Gardens he wrote: "The work was going on night and day. My son John helped superintend. I myself sometimes slept at night on a pile of shavings in the corner of the winter garden when worn out. John would keep going. 'Look here Wright,' said the exasperated Mueller to me one day, 'What's this you got here—this young bull dog that he is. He follows me around and around. Every little while he sticks his teeth in the seat of my pants and I can't get away from him. Can I pull out everything that goes wrong in this work? Can I? Not if I get these gardens finished up, all ready to open on time some day, I can't. Take him off me,' But that sounded good to me and I didn't take him off. John was in it all up to his ears and his teeth were serviceable."

In my father's written account of the Imperial Hotel in Tokio, he did not mention me. He spoke of Paul Mueller and twenty-three architectural students from Japanese Universities, and that was all. When I worked for him in the Midway Gardens, I exerted no independence. No doubt he felt justified in his fury toward me when I worked for him in Japan for it was then that I made a break toward individual liberty, financial and otherwise. But his writings are too widely read for him to indulge himself in such shinanigans. In my anger, I conjured a fiery demon inflamed with the mania for fame extending his conquests over the face of the earth. I saw him contemplate with delight his own dynamic achievements, granting architectural opportunity only to these finite creatures who cast themselves into the abyss of his infinity at the sacrifice of their own individuality. But I got over it.

For eighteen months, John sweat out the work assigned to him as his father's assistant in the Imperial Hotel Project. His job consisted, not in setting his teeth in the seat of Mueller's pants, but in setting his heart in helping his father in the foundation experiments. He took charge of the drafting room, the making of models, and kept a watchful eye on the architect's general interests.

The omission of son's name had repercussions. More than thirty years later, a group of engineers reviewed an application.

Under the heading "past experience" John noted his work for his father in Tokio. He learned that these men called him an impostor, for no mention of him was made in his father's account.

My father's emotions concerning me, at times remind me of W. C. Fields who reportedly, when viewing a performance of Charlie Chaplin, stalked out of the theater before the act was over muttering, "The son-of-a-bitch is a ballet dancer—if I ever get him alone, I'll break his neck."

Should I Change My Name

When I attended the Lloyd-Jones sister's Hillside Home School in Wisconsin, Aunt Nell and Aunt Jenny made it mandatory for each pupil to memorize and recite in turn some motto each morning at breakfast, before sitting down to the oatmeal. This was the bane of my life, for all things that I detested it was recitations of memorizations. I mastered a motto of one line: "O, what a tangled web we weave, when first we practice to deceive." I repeated it at breakfast, each time it came my turn, over a period of six years. Later in life, when I contemplated changing my name, the memory of this motto would plague me. To change my name would certainly not be the solution, but my name has affected me in my dealings with other architects, engineers and men in the construction industry. Right from the start, there has been considerable for me to overcome in this connection. At first, I passed it by with a smile. As time went on I became acquainted with a few facts. Angry hateful emotions toward me were based largely upon resentment toward my father from men who admitted that they did not know me. My name was a red flag.

WHEN I CAME TO CALIFORNIA in 1946 to make my home and work base here, a small group of architects made attacks upon me. A friendly architect conveyed these tidings, "It's too damn bad John but you're in for it, because you're the son of Frank Lloyd Wright." Some members of my profession feel that my name gives me an unfair advantage which throws them into a fugue of fear. The personal motive counteracts this by spreading unfounded rumors about me. This is a problem with which I must cope. There are, of course, many ardent and understanding men in the construction industry who make the going lighter. They are eager to work with me, accepting my name as *my* name.*

TO BE THE SON OF FRANK LLOYD WRIGHT presents a challenge not shared by a son whose father is not a public figure. Fundamentally, both are faced with similar problems, but this son may not escape them. If father is not a public figure and his strength tends to dominate, or his weakness humiliates, son may seek refuge in another city where he enters as a stranger. Not so with this son. The benefits and detriments of his heritage follow him to all corners of the earth. He has had to learn to face up and live with the adulation and the criticism of his fellow men. Adulation and criticism which results from his own activities is not so hard to take. This is the lot of his famous father who voluntarily chose to place his life both personal and professional before the public. But adulation and criticism which results from his father's activities could be a bitter pill. Son John and his father have likenesses, but they have many differences. Son may be strong where his father is weak and weak where his father is strong. But the public judges him as if he were, "a little Frank Lloyd Wright."

IN HIS BOOK, "AS I SAW IT", ELLIOT ROOSEVELT speaks of the drawback of being the son of a famous man but weighs them in the balance, "the rough and the smooth." He tells of his being present at what to him were highly important occasions. It has been my priviledge to be present with my father upon, what to me were, occasions of great moment.

*My father has made the words Architect and Architecture better known. Lillian Gish, the actress, said, in a speech to the A.I.A. Centennial convention in Washington: "You architects remind me of my family, who believes a lady should have her name in the public print just three times—when she is born, when she is married and when she dies. In my lifetime I have heard of only two architects: Frank Lloyd Wright, God bless him for what he has done to make even the word "architecture" known to us; and the other is a memory of my childhood, Stanford White who got shot" (*Architectural Forum*, July 1957).

"SPECIAL PROBLEMS THAT BEFALL A SON"

THE FATE OF THE IMPERIAL HOTEL WAS AT STAKE. It was not the fate of an architectural commission. More important by far, it was the fate of countless numbers of people whose life, limb and property were to be saved from earthquake destruction in the future. The Board of Directors had been frightened by adverse criticism from a California Architect plying his trade in Japan. There was nothing in the engineering books to support my father's design. There is never anything in the books, until some one puts it there.

A conference was called to clear up the fear. It took place between Baron Okura, who represented the Imperial Family's controlling interest and my father, late one night in the Baron's private study in his magnificent Tokio residence. An Interpreter stood by.

I knew my father's professional caution would make it impossible for him to take chances. I knew he was right, for each time a tremor occurred I had measured its effect upon the experimental loaded piles which we had set up on the property. But could he convince the Baron that his conception would work in the complexities of the entire structure? My nerves tingled with anticipation.

The air was tense. It seemed to me that my father was fighting for his life. "We are building on ground which the seismograph shows is never still for a moment, we must prepare to meet it by other means than rigid force," he began. "If there is more awful threat to human happiness than earthquake, I do not know what it can be." There was no movement nor sign of expression on the face of the Baron. "Human beings are maimed, trampled and crushed," my father pleaded, "When without warning a quake comes along it grabs hold of the foundation and snaps it like a whip. We can not fight the quake, we must outwit it." He signaled to me and I spread the drawings on the floor. He explained in detail the plan he had formulated to float the building on the mud cushion, free of the rock strata below, much as a ship floats on water.

Several hours passed. Difficulty after difficulty thinned away. The fate of the Imperial Hotel was determined when Baron Okura

223

rose to his feet and said to my father, "Go ahead, young man."

After the great quake of 1923, when the news was heralded around the world that the Imperial Hotel stood undamaged, my father calmly remarked, "It is the triumph of good sense."

DO MY FATHER'S ACTIONS EMBARRASS ME? When human beings prostrate themselves at his feet and he sits in his king chair absorbing it; when he freely informs the public that everything good in architecture today was done by him first, I am thoroughly embarrassed. I am also embarrassed when questions are asked to evoke an unfavorable opinion from me concerning his architectural work. An impersonal criticism wherein there is disagreement is construed as "sour-grapes," lack of appreciation. Worst of all, I am a disloyal son. If I agree, I'm as crazy as my father. I sense the myopic smugness of the questioner who is certain that I am either too proud to admit my father's errors or too blind to see them. My frustration comes from an inability to explain lest I then be criticized for protesting too much. And so it goes.

THE PROPOSED ARIZONA CAPITOL BUILDING controversy is an example. My father's design is a masterful mural to house the functions of the State Government. The fretted sunlight treatment of roofs and walls does not allow the sun the usual slab surfaces upon which to reflect and bake the life out of everything in sight. It is an oasis such as could not be produced and maintained by nature, in the intense sun of Phoenix.

AMERICAN INSTITUTE OF ARCHITECT'S ETHICS were talked about in the matter of my father's presentation, because other architects had been employed for the project. It looks to me as though his public criticism of their design for the Capitol Building is a jolt in reverse. Perhaps his disrespect for A.I.A. ethics stems from the attack made upon him by one of its illustrious members regarding his design for the Imperial Hotel. There is nothing new in all this. The same things are happening, only to different people.

Turmoil is a foe to the arts and while I deplore it, I understand why my father has been called the "Fujiyama of Architecture." Perhaps his explosions have been of benefit to the public and to Architects from time to time.

"SPECIAL PROBLEMS THAT BEFALL A SON"
Man Brings Forth, After His Kind

Some people say I resemble my father. Some say I inherit his talent. These observations tend to indicate the legitimacy of the relationship. But my heredity is effect, not cause, and in this lies great difference. A more tender regard than mine could no son have for his father. But should I deny that I am the offspring of an infinite system and therefore "one" with all the powers and capacities within that system. Certainly not. If I have felt my father's powerful influence, it is no hereditary legacy. I am convinced that every contemporary architect has felt it too.

Some people say that I am shy. My father's much publicity both early and late in life has influenced my preference to live as far from the pleasurable and painful conflict of spot-lights as he is close to them. This, no doubt, is evidence of my shyness. On the other hand, the late Ernie Pyle was convinced that I am an "unexpurgated edition" of my father. The article in which he expressed this sentiment carried the heading, "John Lloyd Wright's father makes the news today because of his son," Ernie went on to say that I had the same outlook on architecture and the same zealous way of expressing my views as has my father. He made the observation: "John's aggressiveness reached an all-time high in Indianapolis on the occasion of the Architectural Show held at Herron Art Institute. John learned that the hanging committee had consigned his exhibit to the cellar. He rushed to the Herron as fast as he could, found the cellar, rescued his work and defiantly hung it on the wall before the very eyes of the dumbfounded hanging committee. He picked a good place on the wall too. There isn't much more to tell," continued Ernie, "except that Architect Eliel Saarinen, who was the judge that year, crowned John Lloyd Wright with a prize." Ernie did not know that my father is too alert to allow his work to get into the hands of a "hanging committee."

TO CARRY MY FATHER'S NAME is not a one-sided matter. It provides enthusiasm, a warm welcome, be it on train, plane, or public or social gatherings. "Are you a son of Frank Lloyd Wright?" An affirmative reply brings forth recitations of seeing him on T-V, hearing him over Radio, reading his writings, attending his lectures, and there is fascination expressed for his work. The feeling is present that of course son must have some of that stuff in him too. This is a beneficial challenge. "John," said my father one day, "Your father has had to work hard for his recognition, while all you need do is to sign your name." I will go along with that statement if he had in mind a dinner given in his honor forty years ago, to which I was invited because of him.

At this dinner, I drank my first cocktails coupled with the loveliness of an oriental potentate's palace where everything within my vision was exquisite color and form. I am not certain what part of this delicately sensuous beauty was in the rooms and what part was in the cocktails. But I am certain that my special problem that night was to keep from falling flat on my face, while negotiating my way through rooms and corridors to the dinner table.

MEMORABLE are the inspirational hours that I have passed listening to my father's views: ". . . and John,—five lines where three are enough is stupidity. Nine pounds where three are enough is obesity. To know what to leave out and what to put in, just where and just how, ah,—that is to have been educated in the knowledge of simplicity. If you seek simplicity in the spirit, you will never fail to find beauty, though all the gods but One, be against you."

BASICALLY, WHAT MY FATHER'S GENIUS HAS MEANT TO MY LIFE can be summed up in two words: "CHILDHOOD INOCULATION." My eye became accustomed to both rich and simple beauty. The house that was our home had an electrifying quality, an aliveness. The horizontal line had a quieting influence on me. In an extract from his writings my father says, "John being born into it, grew up in the atmosphere of genuine modern architecture without thinking very much about it." I did not need to think much about it. While yet a boy, I watched my father in his creative processes. I knew him intimately, and that was to know the heart of architecture.

My father's activities have attracted the gamut from moron to high-minded person. He heralded into the world the present crop of "Career Architects," who ape his mannerisms first and foremost with equilibrium last and hindmost. One of my special problems, during his flight to fame, was to keep from becoming one of these casualties.

WHEN THE GORDIAN KNOT WAS CUT, I enjoyed my father's peculiar power to charm. I appreciated his ability to strike notes from the heart of life, and I fully realized that to remain with him could well have resulted in an easy life for me. To be a pencil in his hand, to bask in the shadow of his conquests, were all taken into consideration. But,—the boyish ardor was gone and I knew that I must have independence in order to live. My nature required it, demanded it,—come what may. In reality, this son had no choice. He had come to the conclusion that all men, whoever they may be, whatever they have accomplished, are in the final analysis only something among some things. This conclusion has not lightened the special problems that befall this maverick, or is it branded, son.

JOHN LLOYD WRIGHT
5 July 1957

Postscript

My father, John Lloyd Wright, died in California at the age of 80; his wife, Frances, survived him by many years. The absence of a memorial service following his death was consistent with a desire—inherited from his father—to keep the emphasis on the living; and, if he cared little for other details of what happened after he had departed, such as legacies, that too was an attitude he inherited. My father's own life, as my grandfather Frank Lloyd Wright noted, lies partially hidden between the pages of this book, *My Father Who Is on Earth.* Dad's broader work as an accomplished architect, a noted toy manufacturer, and an active member of his community, is another story.

After his death, I archived Dad's drawings at the Chicago Historical Society with the help of Don Kalec of the Frank Lloyd Wright Home and Studio in Oak Park. In 1982, the Historical Society featured a beautiful exhibit of Dad's work curated by the late Ann Van Zanten. The small book published in connection with the exhibition, funded by the Graham Foundation, was, I felt, a valuable documentation of some of my father's most important work.

My father always shared with us—his wife Hazel (our mother) and his children—the places and feeling of his own youth. Our many family visits in the 1930s to Taliesin, Frank Lloyd Wright's home and school in Wisconsin and my father's own childhood residence during his years at the Hillside Home School, evoke strong visual memories: horse carriage rides, Halloween parties, draughting rooms teeming with earnest young students, the work programs, fields of corn, grape vineyards, swimming in the Wisconsin River, picnics, Beethoven wafting through the early morning air, crisp cold nights, and the excitement of thunderstorms with rolling balls of lightning and thunder crashing through the hills. And, if growing to love the evanescent part of nature and respecting the flight of imagination was the point, it worked. For my brother and me, life was stimulating and chal-

228

lenging. My brother became a very talented designer and, until his premature death in his mid-40s from heart disease, he lived a vigorous life. For myself, as an architect, educator, and civic leader, my family gave me the grounds for a creative life—intellectual curiosity, energy, and a belief in the powers of the imagination. There is a tradition of strong women in the family, many of whom were artists, writers, social reformers, and champions of women's rights. It is something of an upsetting irony for me that, in spite of such examples, my father and grandfather shared the old romantic view of women as "beautifully proportioned" helpmates who were supposed to serve their needs and aspirations. Needless to add, we modern independent women have had to reinterpret this role.

In July of 1990, I reread this book—with my grandfather's marginal notes and Dad's responses—at Columbia University where the materials on Wright are archived in the Avery Library. I read with some apprehension, perhaps fearing irreconcilable differences, but my fears were unjustified. I found the comments insightful and often humorous, a setting for things left too long unsaid between father and son, an exchange they both wanted and needed. What was a son's book now becomes a father and son book.

I know Dad was pleased that there was, after all, a thoughtful response from his father. Between them, there was usually so much jest and sidestepping of feelings that neither quite knew what was real and what was fantasy. But I feel that a certain wistfulness about what might have been always characterized their relationship. Dad's encounters with his brothers and sisters were warm but uneven. He trembled, for example, under the hand if not the actual baton of his older brother and colleague, Lloyd, who directed the family orchestra when they were growing up in Oak Park. Later, when Dad was trying to gain reciprocity to practice as an architect in California, Lloyd offered little help. While I know Dad was hurt by the indifference, I feel certain that protocol and form had their day and that family interference would have intensified the battle. In any event, as far as Lloyd and Dad were concerned, their strong independent temperaments made it predictable that they would feel cast into a stormy sea in separate boats; it was less predictable that they would become the splendidly contributive architects that they both became.

I have long been intrigued by certain family patterns. The Lloyd Jones/Wright belief that a strong sense of self worth excuses one from the need to conform to generally accepted rules of social behavior has caused constant personal and public upheaval in the family. Equally unsettling is the carving of a symbol of roots in the earth with the words "truth against the world"—the family motto and symbol—into ancestral fireplace hearths and lintels as if a group of Celtic wizards had passed through. But out of these sensibilities has come the courage, and also the audacity, to ignore the consequences of the inevitable failures in life. I think this has something to do with the condition of creativity. It is easier now for me to see how it came together, generation to generation.

As I read from a few passages in my father's book, I noticed that Frank Lloyd Wright was quick to lash out at anything that suggests that he was grasping the full glory. This was a common theme and criticism against Wright from fellow architects and writers. What I feel we should remember is that Wright wanted to change the course of human affairs—a global mission that was both exasperated and humanized by the familiarity of family and friends. I am reminded here of a recent conference called *The Gathering of Men* which sought to link the support of families to the security needed to expand knowledge. Certainly Frank Lloyd Wright's family provided just such a secure base for his own expansion. My father's struggle was to find this same security.

Another theme that emerges in this book involves the recurrent money problems. My own attitude on this is briefly stated. Money for artists has been, and is, a perennial issue in any economy where artists compete with commercial establishments. It is not surprising to me that an artist—such was the kind of architect that my father was—would find money uncooperative.

In several places in the book, my grandfather suggests that there were reasons other than the Inouye fight or the unpaid salary that contributed to my father's eventual return from Japan to the United States. He was right, there were. On his second trip to Japan, Dad had brought with him his new wife, Jeanette Winters, a dancer from Midway Gardens. It was a stormy marriage that adjusted poorly to Japanese culture. The manager of the Imperial Hotel, an influential figure in the project, advised that Jeanette return home. Given the complexity of the situation, the outcome was star-crossed for Dad who had wanted to continue working with his father on the Japanese projects.

And so it was, father and child caught in an Odyssey. My father fought for independence long after he had it; his identity was clear long before he recognized it. When this book first came out there were those who thought it made light of Frank Lloyd Wright's achievements. In review, I think the story gives us, finally, a "room with a view."

ELIZABETH WRIGHT INGRAHAM

Narciso G. Menocal received both a B.A. and an M.A. from the University of Florida and a Ph.D. from the University of Illinois in the fields of art history and architecture. He is currently a professor in the Department of Art History at the University of Wisconsin. His publications include *Architecture as Nature: The Transcendentalist Idea of Louis Sullivan* and numerous articles on art history and architecture. He is also the editor of *Wright Studies*, a serial published by Southern Illinois University Press.